Tiyan Hanyu Jiaoshi Yongshu

Experiencing Chinese

体验汉语®

国际语言研究与发展中心

小学 • 教师用书
ELEMENTARY SCHOOL
Teacher Book

英文翻译：Harry Gao（美国）

2

高等教育出版社·北京
HIGHER EDUCATION PRESS BEIJING

图书在版编目（C I P）数据

体验汉语小学教师用书. 第2册/国际语言研究与发展中心编著. --北京：高等教育出版社，2010. 12
ISBN 978-7-04-025363-4

Ⅰ. ①体… Ⅱ. ①国… Ⅲ. ①汉语－对外汉语教学－教学参考资料 Ⅳ. ①H195.4

中国版本图书馆CIP数据核字（2010）第028101号

策划编辑 周 芳　　责任编辑 周 芳　　封面设计 高 瓦
插图设计 冰河文化　　责任校对 周 芳　　责任印制 韩 刚

出版发行	高等教育出版社	购书热线	010－58581118
社　　址	北京市西城区德外大街4号	咨询电话	400－810－0598
邮政编码	100120	网　　址	http://www.hep.edu.cn
总　　机	010－58581000		http://www.hep.com.cn
		网上订购	http://www.landraco.com
经　　销	蓝色畅想图书发行有限公司		http://www.landraco.com.cn
印　　刷	廊坊市文峰档案印务有限公司	畅想教育	http://www.widedu.com
开　　本	889×1194　1/16		
印　　张	16.25	版　　次	2010 年 12月第1版
字　　数	480 000	印　　次	2010 年 12月第1次印刷
插　　页	1		

本书如有印装等质量问题，请到所购图书销售部门调换。　　ISBN 978-7-04-025363-4

物料号　25363－00

目录

Contents

附录

Foreword 前言

简介

《体验汉语》小学系列教材由高等教育出版社国际语言研究与发展中心研发，适用于英语国家和地区选修汉语课的小学生，或者5~12岁的汉语学习者。

本系列教材共六册，可供小学1～6年级使用，每个学年一册。每册教材包括一本学生用书（附MP3光盘）、一本练习册（附MP3光盘）、一本教师用书和一套词语卡片。此外，本系列教材还配有一本拼音课本、一套拼音卡片，以及其他多媒体教学资源。

编写理念

本系列教材以“体验式外语教学理念”为编写原则，以学生为主体，话题领先、结构配合，课堂活动和文化活动贯穿全书，目的在于营造快乐的学习气氛，简化汉语学习，激发学习兴趣，使学生具有持续学习汉语的愿望。

为了实现这些目标，编者借鉴并应用汉语作为外语习得与教学的最新研究成果，汲取交际教学法、任务式教学法等各教学法之长，注重本地化原则，遵循“交际、文化、触类旁通、比较和社区” 五个C原则（Communication, Culture, Connection,

INTRODUCTION ▶ The Primary School Textbook Series of Experiencing Chinese is researched and developed by the International Language Research and Development Center of Higher Education Press, suitable for either the English speaking primary school students taking Chinese as elective or the Chinese learners whose age is between 5–12 years.

The textbook series consists of six volumes, servicing grades 1–6. Each volume is designed for the length of one academic school year. Each set of materials includes a copy of Student Book (attached with an MP3 CD), a copy of Workbook (attached with an MP3 CD), a copy of Teacher's Book, and a set of word cards. In addition, the textbook series is provided with a Pinyin Book, a set of Pinyin cards, as well as other multimedia resources.

WRITING RATIONALE ▶ The textbook series takes the “experiencing rationale for foreign language teaching” as the writing principle. Therefore, it centers on students, its topics precede lessons, its structures are coordinated, and both of its class activity and culture activity go through the entire book. The goals are to create a happy learning atmosphere, simplify

Comparison and Community），针对小学生的心理和学习特点，在话题、功能、语音、汉字、词语、句子、语法、语篇、文化、游戏、练习形式等方面都进行了有益的尝试和探索。

◎ 编写特色

本系列教材体现了小学教材的趣味性、科学性和独创性。主要表现在：

1. 内容生动有趣，简单易学，符合少年儿童的年龄特点和心理特点；
2. 课堂活动的种类和数量丰富，强调"在做中学、在玩中学"，符合少年儿童活泼好动的特点；
3. 循序渐进地培养学生"听说读写"四项技能，四项技能在不同级别的教材里各有侧重；
4. 重视学以致用，培养学生将所学知识应用于实际生活的能力，强调"在用中学"；
5. 融合中西方文化，促进跨文化沟通与理解；
6. 触类旁通，建立汉语知识与其他学科知识的关联。

the learning process, stimulate the interest, and keep students' desire to learn Chinese.

To accomplish these goals, the writers have taken reference of and applied the most updated research findings on teaching Chinese as a foreign language, internalized the highlights of the Communicative Approach, Task Oriented Method and other schools of teaching, focused on the principle of localization, followed the five Cs (Communication, Culture, Connection, Comparison and Community), directed at the primary students' psychology and learning styles, and made meaningful trials and explorations in the areas of topics, function, *pinyin*, Chinese characters, sentence, grammar, passage, culture, games, and formats of exercises.

FEATURES ▶ The textbook series reflects the following features in the primary students' teaching materials: fun, scientific and creative. They are visible mainly in:

1. Content is not only vivid and fun, but also simple and easy to learn, suitable for the children and teenagers' age characteristics and psychological characteristics.
2. The class activity is rich in both variety and number. It emphasizes "learning by doing, learning in playing", suitable for the children and teenagers' age characteristics: active and lively.
3. Students' four skills, i.e., "listening, speaking, reading and writing" are cultivated and developed gradually and systematically. They are respectively stressed in the textbooks of different proficient levels.
4. Application is emphasized. Students' practical skills are cultivated through their applying what they've learned in class to their real lives. "Learning through using" is emphatically advocated.
5. Integration of the Chinese and the Western cultures promotes the cross culture communication and understanding.
6. Connection between Chinese knowledge and that of other subjects is established through learning the content of the series.

◎ 课程设计

本系列教材共学习词语552个，补充词语63个，句型56个。主要分为三个阶段。

第❶阶段 ▶ 第一、二册

学习内容：拼音、词语、简单句式和独体字，每两课有一个小故事（看图阅读）。

活动形式：唱歌、做游戏、画画儿、手工制作等

练习册：听、说为主，练习内容主要是拼音、汉字、词语和简单的句子。

词汇与语法：第一册 → 词语62个，句型7个

第二册 → 词语63个，句型8个

第❷阶段 ▶ 第三、四册

学习内容：热身、词语、简单对话和汉字常用笔画，每两课有一个小故事（可以替换故事中的词语）。

活动形式：做游戏、画画儿、手工制作、小表演等

练习册：听、说为主，练习内容主要是拼音、汉字、词语和简单的对话。

词汇与语法：第三册 → 词语79个，

补充词语17个，句型8个

第四册 → 词语82个，

补充词语5个，句型8个

Curriculum ▶ The textbook series teaches a total of 552 words, 63 supplementary words, and 56 sentence patterns. There are three main stages:

STAGE ❶ ▶ Volumes 1 & 2

Content of Study: *pinyin*, words, simple sentence patterns, and independent words. There is a short story in every two lessons (Look at the picture and read)

Activity Formats: singing, *playing games, drawing, handicraft making*, etc.

Workbook: listening and speaking are designed as top priorities. The exercises are primarily focused on *pinyin*, characters, word phrases, and simple sentences.

Vocabulary and Grammar:

Volume 1 → 62 words, 7 sentence patterns

Volume 2 → 63 words, 8 sentence patterns

STAGE ❷ ▶ Volumes 3 & 4

Content of Study: warm up, word and word phrases, simple dialogues, and the common strokes of Chinese characters. There is a short story in every two lessons (Substitutable words provided in the story)

Activity Formats: playing games, drawing, handicraft making, skits, etc.

Workbook: listening and speaking are designed as top priorities. The content of exercises is primarily focused on *pinyin*, characters, word and word phrases, and simple dialogues.

Vocabulary and Grammar:

Volume 3 → 79 words, 17 supplementary words, and 8 sentence patterns

Volume 4 → 82 words, 5 supplementary words, and 8 sentence patterns

第 ❸ 阶段 ▶ 第五、六册

学习内容：热身、词语、较复杂的对话、汉字常用偏旁和汉字结构。每课都有小故事（“读一读”），阅读后需要回答问题。

活动形式：做游戏、制作海报、小调查、课堂讨论等

练习册：听、说、读、写兼顾，练习内容主要是词语、句子、语法、对话、阅读和写作。

词汇与语法：第五册 → 词语138个，
补充词语23个，句型12个
第六册 → 词语128个，
补充词语18个，句型13个

STAGE ❸ ▶ Volumes 5 & 6

Content of Study: warm up, words, comparatively complicated dialogues, radicals of the common Chinese characters and the structures. Every lesson has a short story ("Let's read"). Students need to answer questions after reading.

Activity Formats: play games, make posters, conduct little surveys, and class discussions, etc.

Workbook: listening, speaking, reading and writing are all taken into consideration. The content of exercises is primarily focused on words, sentences, grammar, dialogue, reading and writing.

Vocabulary and Grammar:

Volume 5 → 138 words, 23 supplementary words, and 12 sentence patterns

Volume 6 → 128 words, 18 supplementary words, and 13 sentence patterns.

◉ 感谢

北京教育学院的张静女士参与了本书的编写工作；美国的Harry Gao先生承担了本书的英文翻译工作，在此一并致以诚挚的谢意！

Ms. Zhang Jing from Beijing Education College joined us in compiling this book. Mr. Harry Gao from the United States took upon himself the task of translating this book into English. We extend our heartfelt thanks to both of them.

国际语言研究与发展中心

International Language Research and Development Center

2010年12月

Teacher Manual 使用说明

本书是《体验汉语》小学学生用书第二册的配套教师参考书。

《体验汉语》小学学生用书第二册共有16课，分为相对独立的八个单元，每两课为一个单元。每个单元的主要内容是：

- **单数课**：拼音、拼音练习、课堂活动、词语、词语练习、日常用语
- **双数课**：课文、句型替换、儿歌、句型练习、趣味汉字、文化活动
- **小复习**：游戏、小故事

每个单元的参考教学学时是4~6学时。全书共学习词语63个，句型8个。书后附有1张MP3光盘。

This is the teacher reference book that goes with Experiencing Chinese series for Primary School Students, Student Book, Volume 1.

This book has sixteen lessons, eight relatively independent units. Each unit has two lessons. The highlight of each unit includes:

- **A-Day Class:** *pinyin*, *pinyin* practice, class activity, words, word drill, and daily expressions
- **B-Day Class:** text, sentence pattern substitute, children's song, sentence pattern drill, fun Chinese characters, cultural activity
- **Mini Review:** game, short story

The instructional time for reference teaching section for each unit is 4–6 hours. There are total 62 words, seven sentence patterns in the whole book with one MP3 CD attached.

◉ 本书的主要特点 THE KEY FEATURES OF THE BOOK

● 本书教学步骤讲解清晰，内容丰富，不仅是一本教师用书，也是一本好用的教学参考资料。

The teaching steps in the book are explained clearly, and easy to follow, the content is rich. It's not only a Teacher Manual but also a handy book with reference materials for teaching.

● 本书提供了学生用书第二册里所有练习的录音文本和答案。

The book provides all the recording scripts and keys to the Exercises in the Student Book Vol. 2.

TEA

A Exercise 练一练

Listen and write. 听录音，写一写。

KEY · 答案

ba bai bao ban bang
pa pai pao pan pang
ma mai mao man mang
fa fan fang

B Activity 课堂活动

With two students in a group, count how many b p m f there are on the board. Write the numbers in the circles. 两个小朋友一组，数一数黑板上有多少个 b、p、m、f，把数字写到下边的圆圈里。

方法 ▶▶ 按照学生用书第7页的要求做游戏。教师先领读几次图中卡片上的拼音，随后组织课堂活动：两个学生一组，一起数一数卡片上一共有多少个b、p、m、f，数好后把数字填到图下边的圆圈中。

活动扩展 ▶▶ 教师多准备一些词语卡片，每个卡片上的拼音要包含至少一个b，或者p，或者m，或者f。教师把卡片贴在黑板上，将学生分成几个人数相同的小组，让他们数一数黑板上一共有多少个b，多少个p，多少个m，多少个f。教师记录时间，看哪组数得又快又准确。数得最慢的小组和数错的小组要读出卡片上的拼音。活动时可以随时换掉一些卡片，多次重复这个游戏。

METHOD ▶▶ Do the game after the requirements on page 7 in the Student Book. The teacher leads in reading the *pinyin* on the picture cards, then organizes class activity: two students are in a group. They count together how many b, p, m, f there are on the cards. After they finish the counting, fill the number in the circle underneath the picture.

EXPANDED ACTIVITY ▶▶ The teacher prepares more word cards. The *pinyin* on each card must include at least one b, or p, or m, or f. The teacher puts the cards on the board, and then divides the class into several groups of equal number. Let the students count how many b, p, f, and m in total on the board. The teacher records the time, and decides which group counts both fast and accurately. The slowe... d the mistaken groups ...ave to ... any ti... mes.

● 本书每课都包含一定数量的补充活动，并附有活动页，目的在于方便教师根据学生的汉语水平和实际教学情况灵活地选择教学内容，安排课堂教学。

Every lesson in the book has a certain number of supplementary activities as well as the Activity Pages. The goal of which is to help teachers select the teaching content flexibly and arrange classroom instruction based on the students' Chinese level and the actual teaching situation.

● 本书每页都留有空白处，目的在于方便教师做备课笔记或课堂教学笔记。

Each page in the book has reserved blank space so that the teacher can make notes while planning the lessons.

● 本书为中英文对照，以方便母语为英语的教师使用。

The book is bilingual, written in both Chinese and English so that the teacher whose native language is English can also use it.

● 本书包含学生用书第二册里所有的插图（出现在单数页上，用虚线框起来的部分），目的在于使教师一书在手就能上课教学。

The book has all the pictures in the Student Book Vol.1 (appearing on the odd pages, in the dotted line framed section) so that the teacher can start teaching as soon as he has the book in hand.

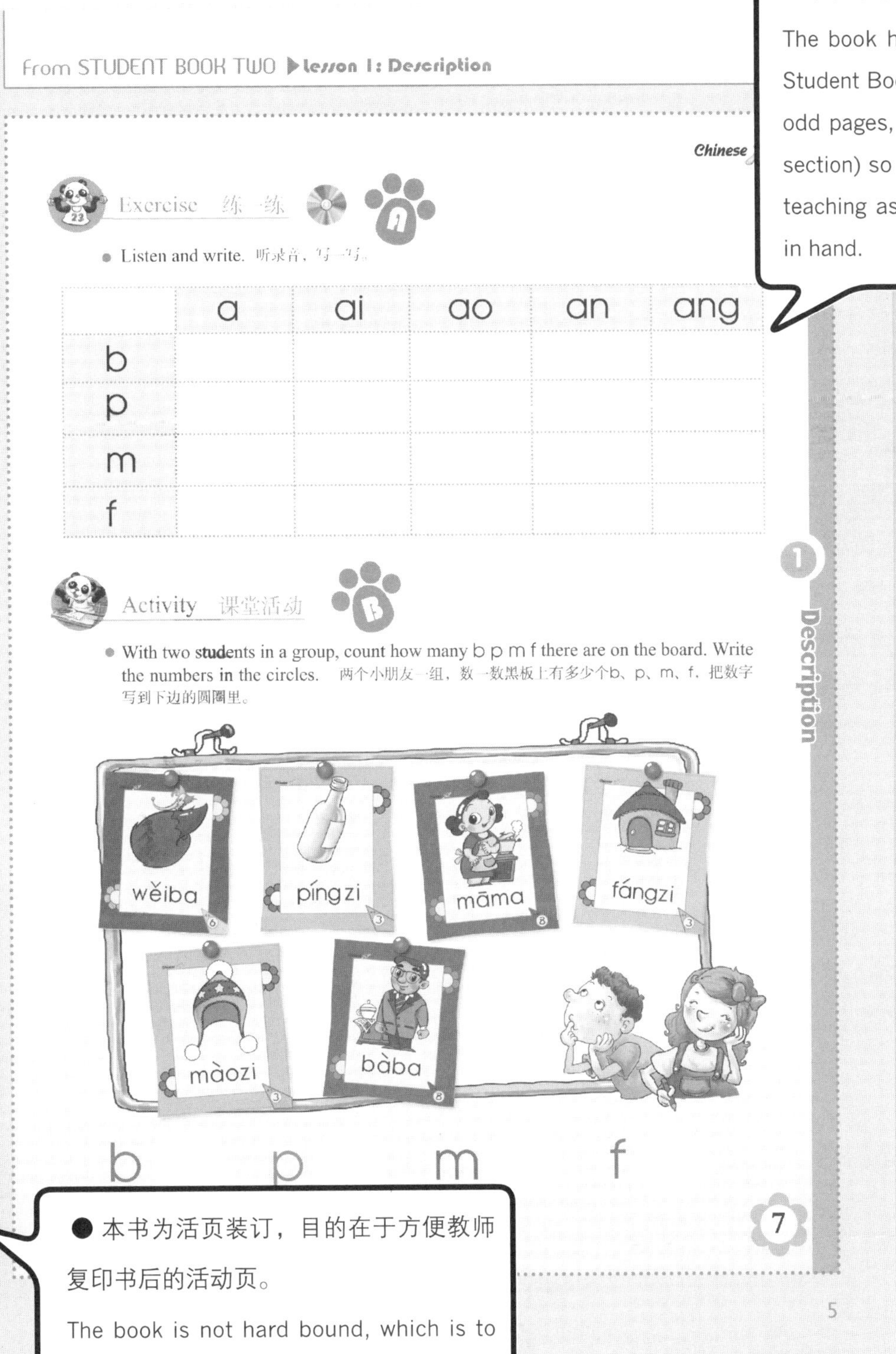
From STUDENT BOOK TWO ▶ Lesson 1: Description

Chinese

Exercise 练一练 A

● Listen and write. 听录音，写一写。

	a	ai	ao	an	ang
b					
p					
m					
f					

Activity 课堂活动 B

● With two students in a group, count how many b p m f there are on the board. Write the numbers in the circles. 两个小朋友一组，数一数黑板上有多少个b、p、m、f，把数字写到下边的圆圈里。

b p m f

1 Description

7

● 本书为活页装订，目的在于方便教师复印书后的活动页。

The book is not hard bound, which is to enable the teacher to make copies off the Activity Pages in the back of the book.

◎ 基本教学方法

学生用书第二册主要内容的教学目的和基本教学方法列举如下：

单数课

读一读 ▶ 这部分学习韵母和声母，以及简单的声韵拼合，附有练习和课堂活动。拼音教学常用的方法包括：

1. 听录音跟读
2. 教师领读，学生跟读
3. 学生全体或者分组朗读
4. 拼音描红
5. 听写或者做听力练习等
6. 朗读儿歌、童谣、绕口令、诗歌等
7. 利用拼音卡片等道具做游戏

认一认 ▶ 这部分学习词语。名词、人称代词用图画表示，动词、虚词等以词条形式展现，配有英文翻译。这部分附有练习和课堂活动。词语教学常用的方法包括：

1. 听录音跟读
2. 教师领读，学生跟读
3. 学生全体或者分组朗读
4. 利用词语卡片做游戏
5. 用英汉互译、看图说词、听词指图等方式做练习

说一说 ▶ 这部分学习简单的日常交际用语。学生能够听说就可以，不要求认读汉字或者写出句子。交际教学常用的方法包括：

1. 听录音跟读
2. 教师领读，学生跟读
3. 教师示范，学生分角色表演
4. 教师在课上课下利用一切机会用所学的句子与学生进行交流

BASIC TEACHING APPROACHES ▶ The major instructional objectives and the basic teaching methods of Student Book, Vol. 2 are:

A-Day Class ▶

Let's read: this section teaches finals and initials as well as simple combinations of initials and finals with exercises and class activities attached. The frequently used methods for *pinyin* instruction include:

1. Listen to the recording and repeat.
2. Teacher leads in reading and students follow.
3. Students read in chorus or groups.
4. Color the *pinyin*.
5. Dictation or listening drill, etc.
6. Read loud the children song, nursery rhyme, tong twister, poem etc.
7. Play games with teaching aids such as *pinyin* cards.

Let's recognize: this section teaches new words. Nouns and personal nouns are illustrated in pictures; verbs and nominal words are expressed in phrases, and with English translation. This section is attached with exercises and class activities. The frequently used teaching approaches for vocabulary include:

1. Listen to the recording and repeat.
2. Teacher leads in reading and students follow.
3. Students read in chorus or group.
4. Play games with word cards.
5. Practice with the methods such as bilingual translation, look at the picture and say sentences, listen to the words and point at the pictures.

Let's say: this section teaches the simple daily social language. Students are not required to identify and read characters or write sentences as long as they are able to understand by listening and respond orally. The frequently used methods for teaching communication skills include:

1. Listen to the recording and repeat.
2. Teacher leads in reading and students follow.
3. Teacher does demo and students perform with different roles.
4. Teacher takes advantage of every opportunity to communicate with students with the sentences learned, either in class or after class.

双数课

学一学 ▶ 这部分学习句型，配有替换练习，替换词为本单元单数课里学习的词语。句型教学常用的方法包括：

1. 听录音跟读
2. 教师领读，学生跟读
3. 教师示范，学生分角色表演
4. 利用词语卡片等道具反复操练句型
5. 用英汉互译、看图说句子、听句子指图等方式做练习

唱一唱 ▶ 这部分以歌曲的方式操练本课句型，学生一边唱歌一边完成任务，潜移默化地掌握本课内容。歌曲中的名词可以用其他同类词替换，进行扩展练习。歌曲教学常用的方法包括：

1. 听录音，学唱歌
2. 教师领唱，学生跟唱
3. 利用词语卡片等道具进行替换和扩展练习
4. 组织表演唱或者唱歌比赛

B-Day Class ▶

Let's learn: this section teaches sentence patterns and is provided with substitute exercises. The words for substitution are the ones covered in the A-Day class in the unit. The frequently used teaching methods for sentence patterns include:

1. Listen to the recording and repeat.
2. Teacher leads in reading and students follow.
3. Teacher does the demo and students perform with different roles.
4. Practice sentence pattern drills repeatedly with the teaching aids such as word cards.
5. Practice with the methods such as bilingual translation, look at the picture and say sentences, listen to the sentences and point at the pictures.

Let's sing: this section practices the sentence patterns in the lesson through singing. Students complete the task while singing songs. They learn the lesson by heart automatically and unknowingly. The nouns in the songs can be substituted with other words of different parts of speech, thus expanding the scope of the exercise. The frequently used methods in teaching songs include:

1. Listen to the recording and learn.
2. Teacher leads in singing and students follow.
3. Conduct substitute and expansion exercises with the word cards and other teaching aids.
4. Organize singing performance and competition.

趣味汉字 ▶ 这部分学写两个简单的独体汉字，目的在于让学生了解汉字的基本笔画、笔顺，掌握正确的下笔方向，为正确书写汉字打下良好基础。汉字教学常用的方法包括：

1. 临摹：教师在黑板上写，学生跟写
2. 描红：在课本上描红
3. 教师示范，用手指在空中写字
4. 学写毛笔字
5. 组织书法比赛

活动 ▶ 活动与每个单元的话题相关。教师可根据指示语和所给的图例引导学生完成这部分的活动。活动常用的方法包括：

1. 教师课前查找资料，课上用幻灯、PPT或实物等展示相关的文化内容，同时用英语简单地介绍相关的情况
2. 教师播放相关的视频资料
3. 教师用英语与学生进行简单的讨论
4. 让学生自己动手，完成手工制作
5. 教师留给学生一些与文化相关的课后任务

复习

❶ **练习**：这部分是一个小游戏，目的在于练习本单元学习的词语或句型。学生根据题目要求做游戏，教师个别检查，给予鼓励或奖励。

❷ **故事会**：这部分是一个连环画故事，目的在于复习本单元学习的句型。有的故事里会出现少量新词，不要求学生掌握，只要能看懂故事的大意或者尝试读出句子即可。这部分常用的教学方法是：

1. 听录音，看故事
2. 教师拿着课本绘声绘色地给学生讲一遍故事
3. 教师用英语与学生讨论故事内容
4. 学生根据故事内容进行小表演

Interesting characters: this section teaches how to write the two simple independent Chinese characters. The goal is to let students understand the basic strokes, order of strokes and master the stroke directions, thus laying a solid foundation for writing the characters correctly. The frequently used methods in teaching character writing include:

1. Copy: teacher writes on the board and students follow.
2. Trace: trace over the characters on the textbooks.
3. Teacher does demo using fingers to write the characters in the air.
4. Learn to write with brush pens.
5. Organize calligraphy contest.

Activity: activity goes through all the topics in each unit. Teacher can guide the students to complete the activity based on the directions and the pictures given. The most frequently used methods for activity include:

1. Teacher searches for materials before the class, uses slides, PPT or real objects to show the relevant cultural content in the class, and briefly introduces the background information in English at the same time.
2. Teacher plays the relevant video materials.
3. Teacher uses English to conduct simple discussions with the students.
4. Let students finish handicraft making on their own.
5. Teacher assigns the home learning task related with the culture.

Review ▶

❶ **Practice:** in this section a little game is played. The purpose is to have students practice the words or the sentence patterns in the unit. Students play game according to the require-

贴心提示

❶ 本书原则上不要求学生掌握拼音和汉字的写法，能够认读即可。但是为了满足不同层次的需求，编者在学生用书和练习册里提供了拼音和汉字描红，教师可以根据所在学校的要求和学生的汉语水平灵活处理。

❷ 教师在做示范、提示或者讲故事的时候，声音、表情、肢体语言等可以夸张一些，以帮助学生理解教师想要表达的内容，吸引学生的注意力。

❸ 教师应想方设法将语言学习与活动、游戏、练习等形式巧妙地结合起来，使后者为前者服务，努力营造快乐的学习气氛，激发学生的兴趣和热情，从而实现“体验汉语，体验快乐，体验成功”的目标。

❹ 欢迎访问我们的网站：www.chinesexp.com.cn，那里将为教师提供更多的教学资源，同时也是一个友好的交流平台。

❺ 在使用《体验汉语》小学系列教材的过程中，如果您有任何问题，请随时与我们联系。专用邮箱：primary2010@163.com

ment of the topic while teacher supervises them individually, giving encouragement or prizes.

❷ **Story time:** this section has a story with a few pictures. The goal is to have students review the sentence patterns covered in the unit. A few new words may appear in the story. Students are not required to master the story as long as they can understand it in a general way or try to read out the sentences. The frequently used teaching methods for this section include:

1. Listen to the recording and read the story.
2. Teacher tells the story vividly with the textbook in hand.
3. Teacher discusses the story with students in English.
4. Students give a little performance based on the story.

Friendly Tips ▶

❶ The principle of the book does not require the students to master *pinyin* and the ways of writing the characters. As long as students can recognize and read them, mission is accomplished. However, the writer provides *pinyin* and tracing over the characters exercises in both the Student Book and the Workbook in order to meet the different levels of need. Teacher can pick and choose flexibly according to the school's expectations and the students' Chinese skill levels.

❷ Teacher can exaggerate voice, expressions, and body language to a certain extent when doing demo, prompting, or telling stories in order to help students understand what the teacher wants to express and attract their attention.

❸ Teacher should try all means to combine language learning with activity, games, and exercises cleverly, making the latter to serve the former, creating a happy atmosphere for learning, stimulating students' interest and enthusiasm, thus reaching the goals of "Experience Chinese, Experience Happiness, Experience Success".

❹ Welcome to visit our website www.chinesexp.com.cn which will provide more teaching materials and platforms for exchange for teachers.

❺ Should you have any questions using Experiencing Chinese series for Primary Schools Students please contact us anytime you wish: primary2010@163.com.

Unit One 第一单元

第一课： 描述

第二课： 我的手很小

教学目标： Objectives
❶ 拼音：b p m f
❷ 句型：……很……

生词： New Words
手 · 嘴 · 头发 · 大 · 小 · 长 · 短

语言点： Language Point
形容词谓语句

日常用语： Daily Expressions
❶ 我是小学生。
❷ A：你读几年级？B：我读二年级。

汉字： Chinese Characters
口 田

活动： Activity
制作手掌画

Introduction 导入

❶ 教师准备一个娃娃或者动物玩偶，也可以以自己的身体为例，一边指着手、嘴、脚、耳朵、头发、鼻子、眼睛等部位，一边用英语或者汉语询问学生："你们还记得这些部位的名称吗？"或者"这是什么？"引导学生用汉语说出他们知道的部位名称。学生说完后，教师指着相关部位，领读几次，学生跟读。复习完部位名称后，教师可以组织两个课堂游戏：（1）"我说你指"游戏：教师走到学生中间，用汉语说出名称，让学生快速指出相应的部位；（2）"我说你不指"游戏：教师用汉语说一个名称，学生不能指相应的部位，也就是听到什么不指什么，如听到"鼻子"，学生要指鼻子以外的部位。

❷ 教师在课前准备一长一短两支笔，一大一小两本书，也可以做一些与"大"和"小"、"长"和"短"有关的图片，如"长头发"和"短头发"、"大苹果"和"小苹果"等。教师举起实物或者图片询问学生这些东西有什么不同，引导学生用英语或者汉语说出"长"、"短"、"大"、"小"。随后教师对比着实物或者图片领读几次这四个形容词，学生跟读，最后教师组织一些简单的课堂练习，如某一位学生领读，其他学生跟读；或者女生领读，男生跟读，等等。

❶ The teacher prepares a doll or an animal puppet, or takes his body parts as examples. While pointing at his body parts such as hand, mouth, foot, ear, hair, nose and eye, he asks the students in English or Chinese: "你们还记得这些部位的名称吗？(Do you still remember the names of these body parts?)" or "这是什么？(What's this?)" to guide the students to speak out the names of these body parts in Chinese. After that, the teacher points at the corresponding body parts and leads in the reading and lets the students repeat after him. After the review, the teacher can organize two class activity games: (1) "I say and you point": the teacher walks among the students, speaks the body parts in Chinese and asks the students to point at the corresponding parts quickly; (2) "I say and you don't point": the teacher speaks a name in Chinese. The students are not allowed to point at the corresponding part, i.e., not to point at the organ they heard. For example, if they hear "鼻子", the students have to point at any other body part but not nose.

❷ The teacher prepares two pens, one long and one short. He can also prepare two books, one large and one small. Or he can make some pictures related to "big" and "small", and "long" and "short", for example "long hair" and "short hair", "big apple" and "small apple", etc. The teacher raises the real objects or the photos to ask the students what differences among them, guiding the students to speak "长（long）", "短（short）", "大（big）", "小（small）" in English or in Chinese. Then the teacher leads in reading these four adjectives with the aid of the real objects or the photos. The students follow the teacher. Finally, the teacher organizes some simple class activities, for example, a student leads in reading, other students follow him; or the girl students lead in reading and the boy students follow, etc.

第1课 描述
miāo shù

Let's read 读一读

Bb bǐ

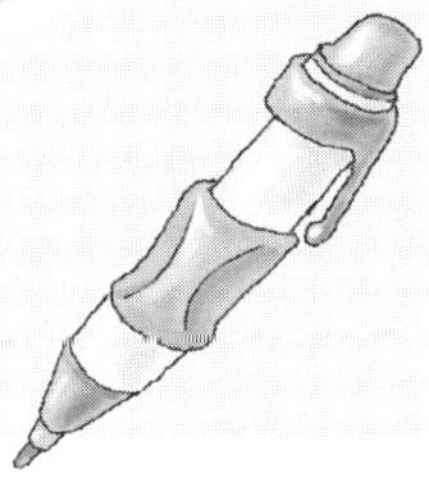

Pp pán

Mm mén

Ff fó

6

Notes

Description 描述 1

Let's read 读一读

❶ 学习声母b、p、m、f的读音。

❷ 学习b、p、m、f与韵母的拼合。

❶ Learn the pronunciations of the initials b, p, m, f.

❷ Learn the combination of the initials b, p, m, f and the finals.

A Exercise 练一练

Listen and write. 听录音，写一写。

KEY · · 答案

ba bai bao ban bang
pa pai pao pan pang
ma mai mao man mang
fa fan fang

B Activity 课堂活动

With two students in a group, count how many b p m f **there are on the board. Write the numbers in the circles.** 两个小朋友一组，数一数黑板上有多少个 b、p、m、f，把数字写到下边的圆圈里。

方法 按照学生用书第7页的要求做游戏。教师先领读几次图中卡片上的拼音，随后组织课堂活动：两个学生一组，一起数一数卡片上一共有多少个b、p、m、f，数好后把数字填到图下边的圆圈中。

活动扩展 教师多准备一些词语卡片，每个卡片上的拼音要包含至少一个b，或者p，或者m，或者f。教师把卡片贴在黑板上，将学生分成几个人数相同的小组，让他们数一数黑板上一共有多少个b，多少个p，多少个m，多少个f。教师记录时间，看哪组数得又快又准确。数得最慢的小组和数错的小组要读出卡片上的拼音。活动时可以随时换掉一些卡片，多次重复这个游戏。

METHOD Do the game after the requirements on page 7 in the Student Book. The teacher leads in reading the *pinyin* on the picture cards, then organizes class activity: two students are in a group. They count together how many b, p, m, f there are on the cards. After they finish the counting, fill the number in the circle underneath the picture.

EXPANDED ACTIVITY The teacher prepares more word cards. The *pinyin* on each card must include at least one b, or p, or m, or f. The teacher puts the cards on the board, and then divides the class into several groups of equal number. Let the students count how many b, p, m, and f in total on the board. The teacher records the time, and decides which group counts both fast and accurately. The slowest and the mistaken groups have to read out the *pinyin* on the cards. Some cards can be replaced at any time during the game. This way the game can be repeated many times.

Exercise 练一练 A

- Listen and write. 听录音，写一写。

	a	ai	ao	an	ang
b					
p					
m					
f					

Activity 课堂活动 B

- With two students in a group, count how many b p m f there are on the board. Write the numbers in the circles. 两个小朋友一组，数一数黑板上有多少个b、p、m、f，把数字写到下边的圆圈里。

b p m f

A Let's recognize 认一认

这部分是本课学习的词语，教学方法参见本书的“使用说明”。

This section teaches the words in the lesson. Refer to the *Teacher Manual* for the teaching method in the book.

SUPPLEMENTARY WORDS [补充生词]

牙 tooth	耳朵 ear	眼睛 eye	鼻子 nose	腿 leg	脚 foot
yá	ěrduo	yǎnjing	bízi	tuǐ	jiǎo

胳膊 arm	肚子 belly	脖子 neck
gēbo	dùzi	bózi

B Exercises 练一练

1. Listen and number the parts of the body. 听录音，填序号。

KEY · · 答案

录音文本：

1. 眼睛　2. 鼻子
3. 嘴　4. 耳朵
5. 手　6. 头发

2. Choose the correct picture according to the word. 根据词语选择正确的图片。

KEY · · 答案

1

Let's recognize 认一认

A

手
shǒu
hand

头发
tóufa
hair

嘴
zuǐ
mouth

大
dà
big

小
xiǎo
small

长
cháng
long

短
duǎn
short

很 hěn very

8

B

Exercises 练一练

1 Listen and number the parts of the body. 听录音，填序号。

2 Choose the correct picture according to the word. 根据词语选择正确的图片。

大
dà

小
xiǎo

长
cháng

短
duǎn

1 Description

9

Notes

Activity 课堂活动

With two students in a group, one points to a picture, and the other one describes the object.
两个小朋友一组，一个小朋友指图片，另一个小朋友说出物品的特征。

方法 按照学生用书第10页的要求做游戏。先让学生自己练习，两个学生一组，一人指图片，另一人用汉语说出物品的特征，教师个别指导。五分钟后，教师组织全班练习，即教师指图片，找学生用汉语说出特征，其他学生跟读，直到全班的学生都得到练习。

词语扩展 根据学生的汉语水平，教师可以带领学生学习更多的形容词，如“多、少”，“高、低/矮”，“粗、细”，“宽、窄”等。

METHOD Do the game after the requirements on page 10 in the Student Book. Have the students practice by themselves first. Divide them into groups of two. One points at the picture and the other speaks out the features of the objects in Chinese. The teacher supervises the students individually. After five minutes, the teacher organizes the whole class for practice, i.e., the teacher points at the picture and calls upon some students to speak out its feature in Chinese. The rest of the class reads after the students. Continue the game till everyone has a chance to practice.

WORDS EXPANSION The teacher can guide the students to learn more adjectives such as “多(duō, many), 少(shǎo, few)”, “高(gāo, tall), 低/矮(dī/ǎi, low/short)”, “粗(cū, thick), 细(xì, thin)” , and “宽(kuān, wide), 窄(zhǎi, narrow)” according to the students’ level of Chinese.

Let’s say 说一说

教学方法参见本书的“使用说明”。

词语替换 学生已经学习过数字1~10，所以对话中的“二年级”可以替换成“一年级”、“三年级”等。

Refer to the *Teacher Manual* for the teaching method in the book.

WORDS SUBSTITUTION Since the students have learned the numbers 1–10, they can substitute “二年级(Second Grade)” in the dialogues with “一年级(First Grade)”, “三年级(Third Grade)”, etc.

1
A
Activity 课堂活动
With two students in a group, one points to a picture, and the other one describes the object. 两个小朋友一组，一个小朋友指图片，另一个小朋友说出物品的特征。
大 dà
小 xiǎo
长 cháng
短 duǎn
10

Let's say 说一说
B
光明小学
我是小学生。
Wǒ shì xiǎoxuéshēng.
I'm a primary school student.
1 你读几年级？
Nǐ dú jǐ niánjí?
Which grade are you in?
2 我读二年级。
Wǒ dú èr niánjí.
I'm in the second grade.
1 Description
11

Notes

Supplementary activities 补充活动

1. Look for the balloons 找气球

准备材料 彩笔、活动页（见附页1.1）

方法 复印活动页，发给每个学生一份。教师在每组三个拼音里随意找一个读出来，学生用彩笔把写有该拼音的气球涂上自己喜欢的颜色。涂好后每个学生分别读一遍自己的答案。完全涂对的学生可以得到一个小奖励。

MATERIALS NEEDED color pens, Activity Page (See attachment 1.1)

METHOD Make enough copies of the Activity Page. Each student receives one copy. The teacher picks one sound out of the three in each group and reads it out. The students then paint the sounds in the balloons with their favorite colors. After that, each student reads out his answers. The students who scores 100% may get a small prize.

2. Listening while writing 边听边写

准备材料 彩笔、活动页（见附页1.2）

方法 两个学生一组，复印活动页，发给每组一份。教师任意说一个部位名称，名称前加上序号，如“1. 鼻子”，两个学生轮流用彩笔在相应的部位上写出序号。做完练习后，教师检查结果，正确的加1分，错误的不加分。得分最高的小组可以得到小奖励。

活动扩展 教师说部位名称，要求学生闭上眼睛用彩笔在活动页图上的相应部位写出序号。

MATERIALS NEEDED color pens, Activity Page (See attachment 1.2)

METHOD Two students are in a group. Make enough copies of the Activity Page. Each group receives one copy. The teacher says randomly the name of a body part, adds a serial number before the name, for example, “1. 鼻子”, the two students write down the serial number at the corresponding position with a color pen by turns. After the practice, the teacher checks the results. The correct one gets one point, the wrong one gets a zero. The group with the highest points may get a small prize.

EXPANDED ACTIVITY The teacher speaks the body parts. The students are required to close their eyes to write down the serial numbers on the corresponding positions with color pens on the pictures on the Activity Page.

3. Say the opposite 正说反做

方法➡此活动的目的是帮助学生掌握几组常用的反义词。这个活动需要大一点的空间，可以在室内或者户外进行。学生站成几排或者围成一圈，教师说一个词语，学生说出它的反义词，同时做出相应的动作，例如教师说“短”，学生说“长”，同时可以伸开双臂做出“长”的动作。

扩展活动➡教师找一名学生到前边，教师背对着全班同学，给前边的学生看一张词语卡片，如“大”，前边的学生根据词语卡片做出相反的动作，即做出“小”的动作，其他同学猜一猜卡片上的词是什么。

参考词语➡长/短、多/少、大/小、高/低、高/矮、上/下、左/右、粗/细、宽/窄

METHOD➡The goal of this activity is to enable the students to learn the several groups of the opposites frequently used. It requires a bigger space for the activity. It can be done either indoors or outdoors. The students stand in several lines or in a circle. The teacher says a word and the students respond with its opposite with the corresponding gesture. For example, the teacher says “短”, the students respond with “长”, and extend their arms to indicate the length.

EXPANDED ACTIVITY➡The teacher asks a student to come to the front. The teacher shows a word card to the student with his back to the class, for example, “大”. The student makes an action opposite the meaning of the word on the card, i.e., an action indicating “小”, and let the class guess the word on the card.

REFERENCE WORDS➡long/short, many/few, big/small, high/short, high/low, up/down, left/right, thick/thin, wide/narrow

2 My hands are small 我的手很小

A Let's learn 学一学

❶本课学习由“很”构成的形容词谓语句，基本格式是“主语+很+形容词”。本课中的主语由“名词/代词+的+名词”构成，如“我的头发”，“妈妈的手”等。

❷教师先准备一本大大的书和一本小小的书，通过对比让学生说出词语“大”和“小”，随后教师一边举书一边领学生说句子：“书很大”，“书很小”。学生理解了句子的意思以后，教师快速举起大书或者小书，找学生独立说出句子。

❸教师可以组织一个课堂活动。教师准备大小不同或者长短不一的两个实物或者两张卡片，如一大一小两个苹果，一长一短两根铅笔。教师拿其中的一个，另一个给某个学生。教师先说“我的苹果很小”，学生接着说“我的苹果很大”，教师引导其他学生跟着复述：“老师的苹果很小”，“××的苹果很大”。也可以叫两个学生到前边，把实物或者卡片分别给学生，让学生根据实物或卡片说出句子，其他学生复述。

❹教师让学生打开书，看图，听录音，跟读课本中的句子。这部分配有替换词语，可以用来进行替换练习。练习之前教师把句型“我的……很……”写在黑板上，然后教师指着替换部分的第

❶ This lesson teaches the predicative sentence with “很”. The basic sentence pattern is “subject +很+ adjective”. The subjects in the lesson consist of “noun/pronoun + 的 +noun”, for example, “我的头发”, “妈妈的手”, etc.

❷ The teacher prepares a super large book and a tiny little book beforehand. Have the students say “大” and “小” through comparison, and then the teacher leads the students to say the sentences: “书很大”, “书很小”. Based on the students' understanding of the sentence, the teacher raises the big or the small book quickly and let the students say the sentences.

❸ After that, the teacher may organize a class activity. The teacher prepares two real objects of different sizes and lengths or the photos of such objects. For example, two apples, one is big and the other is small; two pencils, one is long and the other is short. The teacher holds one of them, gives the other one to a student. The teacher says first, “我的苹果很小”. The student carries it on, “我的苹果很大”. The rest of the class repeats: “老师的苹果很小”, “××的苹果很大”. The teacher can also call two students to the front, gives them either the real objects or the cards. Have

第2课 我的手很小

wǒ de shǒu hěn xiǎo

Let's learn 学一学

一幅图做示范，用粗一点的声音模仿鳄鱼说：“我的嘴很大！”让学生跟着模仿。随后教师任意指一幅图，让几个学生试着说出句子。学生说完后，教师说一遍正确的句子，全班学生跟读。教师也可以引导学生用“我/××（同学或者老师的名字）的……很……”说出自己或别人的手、脚、头发等身体部位的特征。

them speak out the sentences after the real objects or the cards. The rest of the class repeats.

❹ The teacher asks the students to open their books, look at the pictures, listen to the recording, and follow the sentences in the textbook. This section is provided with the substitute words which can be used for the substitution drills. Before the practice, the teacher writes down the sentence pattern “我的……很……” on the board, and then points at the first picture in the substitution section to do a demo, using a bit hoarse voice to imitate a crocodile: “我的嘴很大！” Have the students imitate. Then the teacher points at a picture and asks the students to try to say the sentence. After that, the teacher says the sentence once and correctly, and the whole class reads after the teacher. The teacher can also guide the students in using “我/XX(classmates or teacher’s names) 的……很……” to speak the features of his own or the other people’s body parts such as hand, foot or hair.

TEXT TRANSLATION [课文译文]

我的手很小。My hands are very small.

爸爸的手很大。Dad’s hands are very big.

PATTERN’S SUBSTITUTE [句型替换]

我的嘴很大。　我的嘴很小。

我的头发很长。　我的头发很短。

Let's try 试一试

______的______很______。

de　　　hěn

zuǐ (dà)

zuǐ (xiǎo)

tóufa (cháng)

tóufa (duǎn)

A Guess and sing 猜一猜，唱一唱

歌曲的学习方法参见本书的“使用说明”。

活动方法➡学生们学会歌曲以后，教师组织课堂活动：学生们围成一圈，让学生A站到中间，闭上眼睛，教师和学生B分别去拉一下学生A的手，同时大声说：“这是我的手”。学生A根据声音猜出答案：“这是老师/××的手”。猜对后，学生A睁开眼睛，老师和学生B分别站到学生A的旁边，学生A拉着老师和学生B的手，带领全班同学一起唱歌。本课歌曲中的人名可以随意替换。

歌曲文本➡这是老师的手。这是老师的手。老师的手很大。大大大大大大。这是美美的手。这是美美的手。美美的手很小。小小小小小小。

Refer to the *Teacher Manual* for the method for learning the song in the book.

ACTIVITY METHOD➡After the students have learned how to sing the song, the teacher then organizes the class activity: have the students stand in a circle. Let Student A stand in the middle, and close his eyes. The teacher and Student B go and pull Student A's hands, and say the sentence “这是我的手” simultaneously. Student A makes a guess based on the voice: “这是老师/××的手”. If he guesses right, Student A opens his eyes. The teacher and Student B step aside of A. Student A holds both the teacher's and Student B's hands, and lead the whole class to sing in chorus. The names of the song in the lesson can be changed at will.

THE SONG SCRIPT➡This is teacher's hand. This is teacher's hand. Teacher's hand is very big. Big big big big big big. This is Meimei's hand. This is Meimei's hand. Meimei's hand is very small. Small small small small small small.

B Sentence patterns 学句型

Read the patterns aloud, and then look at the pictures and compose sentences with “很”. 大声朗读句型，然后看图用“很”造句。

❶ 这部分是句型总结与复习。教师先领学生反复大声朗读句型框里的句型，直到学生可以流利地读出句型框里的四个句子。

❶ This section is the summary of the sentence patterns and reviews. The teacher first leads the students in reading aloud the sentence

2

Guess and sing 猜一猜，唱一唱

A

Zhè shì lǎoshī de shǒu.
Zhè shì lǎoshī de shǒu.
Lǎoshī de shǒu hěn dà.
Dà dà dà dà dà dà.

Zhè shì Měiměi de shǒu.
Zhè shì Měiměi de shǒu.
Měiměi de shǒu hěn xiǎo.
Xiǎo xiǎo xiǎo xiǎo xiǎo xiǎo.

14

Sentence patterns 学句型

B

- Read the patterns aloud, and then look at the pictures and compose sentences with “很”. 大声朗读句型，然后看图用“很”造句。

我的嘴 wǒ de zuǐ	很 hěn	大 dà
我的嘴 wǒ de zuǐ		小 xiǎo
我的裙子 wǒ de qúnzi		长 cháng
我的裙子 wǒ de qúnzi		短 duǎn

____

____

____

____

2 My hands are small

15

Notes

❷ 学生看图，用“我的……很……”造句，可以用拼音或者汉字写出答案，教师个别指导。学生做完练习后，教师找学生分别模仿动物的声音把自己写的答案读出来。如果学生的汉语水平较高，教师可以把“我”换成动物的名称，即“鹦鹉”、“松鼠”、“猴子”、“兔子”。

patterns in the sentence pattern frame repeatedly till they can read the four sentences in the box fluently.

❷ Looking at the picture, the students use “我的……很……” to make up sentences, and write down the answers in Pinyin or Chinese characters. The teacher supervises the students on the individual basis. After the students are done with the practice, the teacher chooses the students to mimic the animal sounds and read aloud the answers written by themselves. If the students know more Chinese, the teacher can change “我” into animals' names such as “鹦鹉(parrot)”, “松鼠(squirrel)”, “猴子(monkey)” and “兔子(rabbit)”.

KEY · · 答案

我/鹦鹉的眼睛很大。　我/松鼠的眼睛很小。

我/猴子的尾巴很长。　我/兔子的尾巴很短。

A Interesting characters 趣味汉字

本课学习的汉字是“口”和“田”，要求学生掌握这两个字的正确写法。汉字的教学方法参见本书的“使用说明”。

This lesson teaches the characters “口” and “田”. The students are required to master the correct way of writing these two characters. Refer to the *Teacher Manual* for the teaching method in the book.

B Let's do it 做一做

准备材料 彩笔、剪刀、纸、颜料或者印泥

方法 用三种方法画出自己的手。方法一：把手放在纸上，用彩笔沿着手的边缘画出手的轮廓，在轮廓内涂上颜色，然后用剪刀剪下来。方法二：用颜料或者印泥把自己的手印在纸上。方法

MATERIALS NEEDED color pens, scissors, paper, paint or stamp ink

METHOD Use three methods to draw your hand. Method 1: put your hand on a piece of paper; use the color pens to draw along the edges of your hand. Then paint it with colors. Finally, cut it out with a pair

2
Interesting characters 趣味汉字
A
口
mouth
kǒu
田
earth
tián
16

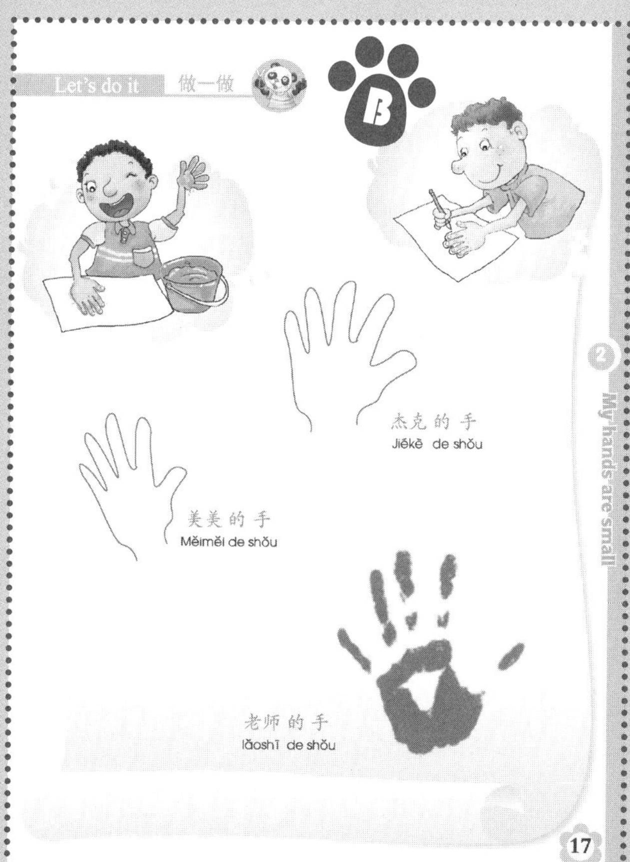
Let's do it 做一做
B
杰克的手
Jiékè de shǒu
美美的手
Měiměi de shǒu
老师的手
lǎoshī de shǒu
2 My hands are small
17

Notes

三：两人一组，用不同颜色的彩笔在同一张纸的同一个位置上分别画出各自的手，然后比较一下有什么区别。手掌画做完后，在纸上写上自己的名字，如“××的手”，然后做一个漂亮的墙报。

of scissors. Method 2: put the paint or the stamp ink on your palm, and then put your palm on a piece of paper. Method 3: two students are in a group. Use the pens of different colors to draw one's hand on the same location and on the same paper. Then compare to see what differences are there between the two hands. After the palm picture is finished, write one's name on the paper, for example, "××的手", and then make a pretty wall paper.

Supplementary activities 补充活动

1. Arrange sentences with the characters 汉字拼句

准备材料 ➡ 剪刀、活动页（见附页2.1）

方法 ➡ 复印足够数量的活动页，发给每个学生一份。学生把表格中的汉字和标点符号逐个剪下，拼出所给的四个句子，拼好后举手，教师走到学生身边，学生大声把四个句子朗读出来。

MATERIALS NEEDED ➡ scissors, Activity Page (See attachment 2.1)

METHOD ➡ Make copies of the Activity Page. Each student receives one copy. Have the students cut out the Chinese characters and the punctuations in the form, and then arrange the characters into the four sentences given. After done, the student raises his hand to get the teacher's attention. The teacher then comes to the student, and the student reads aloud the four sentences.

2. Look for the same picture 找相同

准备材料 ➡ 活动页（见附页2.2）

方法 ➡ 学生两人一组，一人拿A图，一人拿B图，互相不能看对方的图。教师提示学生在两张图中只有一幅小图完全一样，其他小图都有不一样的地方，要求学生按照所给例句通过对话找出相同的小图画。

MATERIALS NEEDED ➡ Activity Page (See attachment 2.2)

METHOD ➡ Two students are in a group. One holds Picture A and the other holds Picture B. They can't look at each other's picture. The teacher reminds the students that there is only one drawing in each picture that is identical, and the rest of the

对话示例

××的……很……

A：美美的裙子很长。

B：美美的裙子很短。

答案：鸟

drawings all have different places. The students are required to find the identical drawings from the two pictures through dialogue according to the example.

EXAMPLES See the Chinese version on the left.

3. Look and paste 找一找，粘一粘

准备材料 剪刀、胶棒、活动页（见附页2.3）

方法 复印足够数量的活动页，发给每个学生一份，包括一张物品图和一张人物图。学生先把物品图上的物品剪下来，随后教师根据物品图上的事物说句子，如“她的头发很长”，“猫的尾巴很短”。为了让学生听明白，每个句子可以多重复几遍。学生一边听一边对应的物品粘贴在人物图上的相应位置上。贴好后，学生试着用中文描述人物图上的人和事物。

参考句子

她的头发很长/短。

苹果很大/小。

电脑很大/小。

她的嘴很大/小。

笔很长/短。

她的手很大/小。

她的裙子很长/短。

猫的尾巴很长/短。

书很大/小。

MATERIALS NEEDED scissors, glue stick, Activity Page (See attachment 2.3)

METHOD Make copies of the Activity Page. Each student receives one copy, including a picture of people and a picture of objects. The students first cut out the objects from the object picture, and then the teacher starts to say sentences according to the objects from the picture of objects, for example, “她的头发很长”, “猫的尾巴很短”. In order to make the students understand, the teacher can repeat the sentence several times. The students then paste the corresponding object onto the picture of the people till the picture is finished. Finally have the students describe the picture of people in Chinese.

REFERENCE SENTENCES See the Chinese version on the left.

REVIEW | 复习

A Draw and write 画一画，写一写

准备材料➡ 彩笔

方法➡ 按照学生用书第18页的要求做练习。学生先用彩笔为图片中的白色部分涂上自己喜欢的颜色，然后根据图画完成填空，可以写拼音也可以写汉字。完成后，两个人一组互相检查，教师个别指导。

MATERIALS NEEDED➡ color pens

METHOD➡ Do the exercise after the directions on page 18 in the Student Book. With the color pens, the students first paint their favorite color on the white parts of the pictures, and then fill in the blanks according to the picture. It can also be done with *pinyin* or the characters. When they finish the work, the teacher can have the two students in a group to check each other's work. The teacher supervises the students on the individual basis.

B Story time 故事会

教学方法参见本书的"使用说明"。

故事文本➡ 一只小老鼠在房间里看到一面哈哈镜。它上前照了照，看到哈哈镜里面的自己又高又大，所以它很骄傲地对自己的同伴说："我很大！"这时候，一只猫走了过来。老鼠们看到猫，吓得四处躲藏，只有小老鼠还在骄傲地说："我很大！""喵！"猫一下子用爪子按住了它。小老鼠看到猫，吓了一跳。它这才明白它没有那么大，它叹口气："我真小！"

Refer to the *Teacher Manual* for the teaching method in the book.

STORY TEXT➡ A little rat sees a distorting mirror in the room. She goes up and takes a look. She sees herself not only tall but also big. So she is very proud to tell her fellow friends: "我很大！" Then a cat walks by. The rats are scarred away except this little rat still repeating: "我很大！" with pride. "Mew!" Suddenly the cat catches the rat with his paws. The little rat gets startled when she sees the cat. Only then has she realized that she is not that big. "我真小！" she sighs.

TRANSLATION[译文]➡ 图2：我很大！I am very big.
图3：我很大！I am very big.
图4：我真小！I am so small.

Review 1（复习1）

1 Draw and write 画一画，写一写

Niǎo de ____ hěn ____

Bào de ____ hěn ____

Māma de ____ hěn ____

Wǒ de ____ hěn ____

Húdié de ____ hěn ____

Lǎoyīng de ____ hěn ____

18

2 Story time 故事会

19

Notes

Notes

Unit Two 第二单元

第三课：称赞
第四课：他们真棒

教学目标： Objectives
❶ 拼音：d t n l
❷ 句型：……真……

生词： New Words
可爱 · 聪明 · 漂亮 · 帅 · 好 · 棒 · 真 · 它们

语言点： Language Point
感叹句

日常用语： Daily Expressions
A：我学习汉语。你呢？
B：我学习西班牙语。

汉字： Chinese Characters
儿 七

活动： Activity
听一听，做动作

Introduction 导入

❶ 教师准备几张与“大”和“小”、“长”和“短”有关的玩具或者图片，如“大鱼”和“小鱼”、“长尾巴猴子”和“短尾巴熊猫”等，引导学生用“……很……”说出动物的特征。随后教师领读正确的句子，学生跟读，以此复习前一单元学习的内容。

❷ 教师在课前准备一些表示“漂亮”、“帅”、“可爱”、“聪明”、“棒”的图片，如学生喜欢的电影明星、体育明星、科学家，以及可爱的小动物、婴儿等。教师依次展示这些图片，同时用夸张的表情和语气说：“真漂亮！”“真帅！”“真聪明！”“真可爱！”“真棒！”随后教师再次展示这些图片，同时问学生：“你喜欢他吗？为什么？”引导学生用英语或者汉语说出“漂亮”、“帅”等词语。最后教师举卡片领读词语，学生跟读。

❶ The teacher prepares a few toy pictures showing “big” and “small”, “long” and “short”, such as “big fish” and “small fish”, “ a monkey with a long tail” and “a panda bear with a short tail” etc, guiding the students to use “……很……” to speak out the features of the animal. Then the teacher leads in reading the correct sentences and the students follow him. Through this way the lessons in Unit One get reviewed.

❷ The teacher prepares some pictures expressing the concepts of “pretty”, “handsome”, “lovely”, “smart”, “super” etc before the class, such as the students’ favorite movie stars, sports stars, scientists, cute pets and babies. The teacher shows these pictures in turn and says “真漂亮！”“真帅！”“真可爱！”“真棒！” with the exaggerated facial expression and tone. Then the teacher shows these pictures one more time, and asks the students, “你喜欢他吗？为什么？(Do you like him? Why?)” The goal is to guide the students to say “漂亮”, “帅” etc. in either English or Chinese. Finally, the teacher raises the cards and leads in reading the words with the students following him.

Notes

第3课 称赞
chēng zàn
Let's read 读一读

Dd dòu
Tt tú
Nn niú
Ll lóu

20

Notes

Praise 称赞

Let's read 读一读

❶ 学习声母d、t、n、l的读音。

❷ 学习d、t、n、l与韵母的拼合。

❶ Learn the pronunciations of writing of the initials d, t, n, l.

❷ Learn the combination of the initials d, t, n, l and the finals.

A Exercise 练一练

Listen and mark the tones. 听录音，标声调。

KEY · · 答案

dā dàn diàn liē léi
diū duì tuó tǒng

B Activity 课堂活动

With two students in a group, point out the initials you hear. 两个小朋友一组，指出听到的声母。

方法 按照学生用书第21页的要求做游戏。教师把d、t、n、l 四张拼音卡片贴在黑板上，然后拼出带有d、t、n、l 中任意一个声母的拼音，例如l-óu-lóu，学生根据教师的发音找出声母，并跑到黑板前指出相应的拼音卡片。

活动扩展1 将学生分成两组，每组每次派一个学生上前指出声母，先指对的学生所在的小组得1分。每个学生都得到练习后，教师统计一下两组的得分，得分多的一组获胜。

活动扩展2 教师课前从本书第一册、第二册的卡片里选取一些拼音里包含有d、t、n、l 的词语卡片，分给学生每人一张。教师任意指黑板上 d、t、n、l 中的一个声母，如 d，拿着包含 d 的词语卡片的学生把卡片举起来，并试着读出卡片上的拼音。

参考拼音

1. l—óu—lóu
2. t—ā—tā
3. n—ǐ—nǐ
4. d—ì—dì
5. t—īng—tīng
6. n—ǎi—nǎi
7. l—ù—lù
8. d—à—dà

METHOD Start the game after the directions on page 21 in the Student Book. The teacher puts the four spelling cards with d, t, n, l on the board and then says a sound with any of the four initials, for example, l-óu-lóu. The students look for the initials according to the teacher's pronunciations, run to the board and point at the corresponding cards upon finding them.

EXPANDED ACTIVITY 1 Divide the students into two groups. Each group sends one student to the front to identify the initials each time. The group that is first in finishing the task correctly gets one point. After every student gets a chance to practice the teacher tallies the points from the two groups. The group with the higher points wins in the end.

EXPANDED ACTIVITY 2 The teacher selects some of the word cards containing the initials d, t, n, l from Book 1 and Book 2 before the class. Each student receives one card. The teacher points randomly at any one of the four initials on the board, for example, d, then the student with the d card raises the card and tries to sound it out.

Exercise 练一练

A

- Listen and mark the tones. 听录音，标声调。

ˉ ˊ ˇ ˋ

da dan dian lie lei

diu dui tuo tong

Activity 课堂活动

B

- With two students in a group, point out the initials you hear. 两个小朋友一组，指出听到的声母。

A Let's recognize 认一认

这部分是本课学习的词语，教学方法参见本书的“使用说明”。

This section teaches the words in the lesson. Refer to the *Teacher Manual* for the teaching method in the book.

SUPPLEMENTARY WORDS[补充生词]

酷 kù cool | 好看 hǎokàn pretty | 调皮 tiáopí naughty | 淘气 táoqì mischievous

B Exercises 练一练

1. Listen, number the words, and then match. 听录音，填序号，连一连。

KEY · 答案

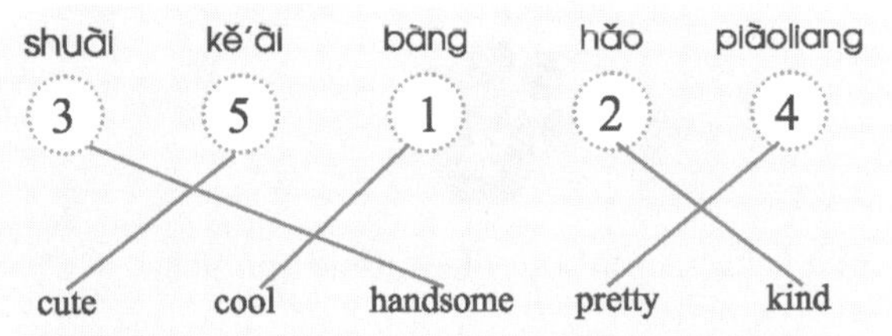

录音文本：

1. 棒　　2. 好
3. 帅　　4. 漂亮
5. 可爱

2. Arrange the letters and write the *pinyin* for the words. 排一排，写出正确的拼音。

KEY · 答案

kě'ài　wǒmen　cōngming　piàoliang

3

Let's recognize 认一认

A

可爱
kě'ài
cute

聪明
cōngming
smart

漂亮
piàoliang
pretty

帅
shuài
handsome

好
hǎo
kind

棒
bàng
cool

真	zhēn	so
它	tā	it
们	men	(the plural form for human and animal)

我们	wǒmen	we, us
你们	nǐmen	you
他们	tāmen	they, them (for male)
她们	tāmen	they, them (for female)
它们	tāmen	they, them (for nonhuman creature)

22

B

Exercises 练一练

1 Listen, number the words, and then match. 听录音，填序号，连一连。

shuài kě'ài bàng hǎo piàoliang

cute cool handsome pretty kind

2 Arrange the letters and write the *pinyin* for the words. 排一排，写出正确的拼音。

ě k ài
可爱 ________

w en m ǒ
我们 ________

c ing ōng m
聪明 ________

ào i p l ang l
漂亮 ________

3 Praise

23

Notes

A Activity 课堂活动

Remember and say. 记一记，说一说。

准备材料 “可爱”、“聪明”、“漂亮”、“帅”、“好”、“棒”六个词的词语卡片，以及与卡片大小相同的六张白纸。

方法 按照学生用书第24页的要求做游戏。教师把六张词语卡片贴在黑板上，给学生10秒钟的时间记住每张卡片的位置，随后教师用透明胶把白纸粘在卡片上。教师任意指一张卡片，让学生根据记忆猜出卡片上的词语。没猜对的话，教师说“不对，再试试！”鼓励学生继续猜。学生猜对后，教师说：“对了！非常好！太棒了！”然后揭开白纸，跟学生一起读出卡片上的词语。

活动扩展 找六个学生到黑板前，每人举一张卡片，展示10秒钟后把卡片藏到身后，其他学生猜词语。重复这个游戏，直到全班学生都得到练习。

MATERIALS NEEDED Prepare for the six words: “可爱”, “聪明”, “漂亮”, “帅”, “好” and “棒”, as well as six pieces of blank white paper of the same size as the cards.

METHOD Start the game after the directions on page 24 in the Student Book. The teacher pastes the six word cards on the board. Give the students 10 seconds to memorize the positions of each card. Then the teacher uses the transparent tape to cover the cards with the pieces of the white paper. The teacher points at a card randomly and asks the students to guess out the words on the card by memory. If the student is wrong, then the teacher says: “不对，再试试！(Not right. Try one more time!)” to encourage the student to continue guessing. When the student's guess is correct, the teacher says: “对了！非常好！太棒了！(Right! Super good! Really super!)” Then the teacher uncovers the pieces of the white paper and reads the words on the cards with the students.

EXPANDED ACTIVITY Choose six students and ask them to go to the front. Each carries a card. After 10 seconds of showing the words on the cards, the students hide them behind their backs. The rest of the class starts to make guesses. Repeat the game till all the students have a chance to practice.

B Let's say 说一说

教学方法参见本书的“使用说明”。

补充词语 中国—汉语　美国—英语　加拿大—英语　英国—英语　澳大利亚—英语　日本—日语　韩国—韩语　泰国—泰语　法国—法语　意大利—意大利语

Refer to the *Teacher Manual* for the teaching method in the book.

SUPPLEMENTARY WORDS China-Chinese The U.S.-English Canada-English Britain-English Australia-English Japan-Japanese South Korea-Korean Thailand-Tai France-French Italy-Italian

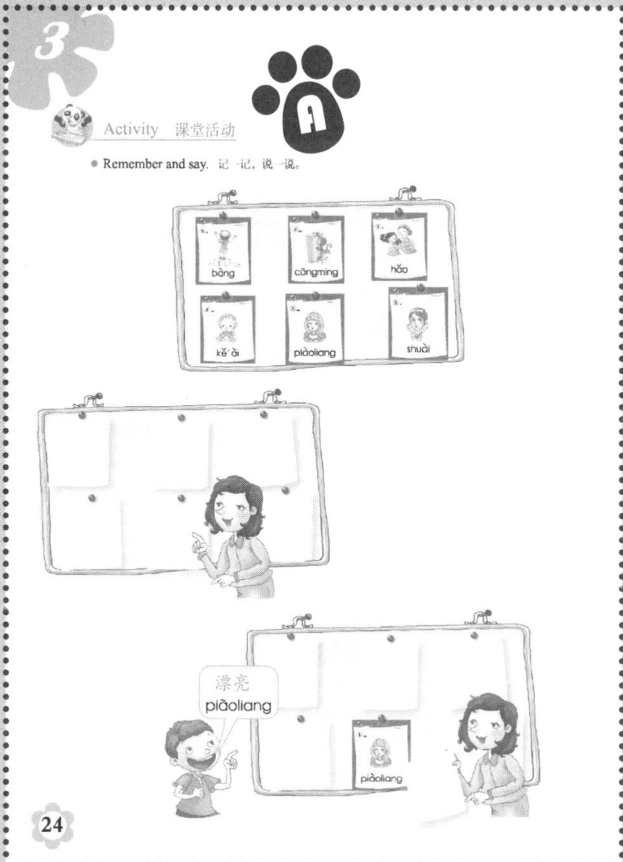
3
A
Activity 课堂活动
Remember and say. 记一记，说一说。
bàng
cōngming
hǎo
kě'ài
piàoliang
shuài
漂亮
piàoliang
piàoliang
24

Let's say 说一说
B
1 我学习汉语。你呢？
Wǒ xuéxí Hànyǔ. Nǐ ne?
I study Chinese. How about you?
2 我学习西班牙语。
Wǒ xuéxí Xībānyáyǔ.
I study Spanish.
3 Praise
法语
Fǎyǔ
French
英语
Yīngyǔ
English
日语
Rìyǔ
Japanese
25

Notes

Supplementary activities 补充活动

1. Raise the cards 举卡片

准备材料 根据学生数量，准备一些拼音卡片（包括本课学习的声母d、t、n、l）和四张声调卡片。

方法 教师把卡片分发给学生，每个学生一张。教师说一个音节，如dà，然后数"1－2－3"，在数到"3"的时候，持有卡片d，a和四声声调的学生一起举起卡片并读出拼音。正确举出卡片的学生加1分，超时或者举错的不加分。学生可以自己在纸上计分。学生们互相交换卡片，教师说一个新的拼音，重复该游戏。游戏完成后，得分最高的前三名学生得到小奖励。

MATERIALS NEEDED Prepare enough *pinyin* cards according to the number of the students in the class (including the initials d, t, n, l learned in the lesson) and four tonal cards.

METHOD The teacher gives the cards to the students. Each receives one card. The teacher starts to say a *pinyin*, for example, dà. After that the teacher begins to count "1-2-3". At "3", the students who hold the cards d, a and the fourth tone raise their cards and read out the *pinyin*. The correct students get one point; the students who miss or display the wrong one get no point. The students can keep the points on the paper by themselves. Then the students exchange cards. The teacher starts to say a new *pinyin* to repeat the game. The top three scorers will get small prizes.

2. Look for friends 找朋友

准备材料 活动页（见附页3.2）

方法 复印足够数量的活动页，发给每个学生一份。根据学生的学习情况规定一个时间，如五分钟，让学生把可以组成词语的汉字连在一起，然后把这个词的拼音写出来。在规定的时间内看谁做得又好又快。

MATERIALS NEEDED Activity Page (See attachment 3.2)

METHOD Make enough copies of the Activity Page. Each student receives one copy. Make a deadline according to the students' learning situation, for example, five minutes. Have the students arrange the characters which can make words when combined together, and then write down the *pinyin* of the words. Compete to see who finishes the task first and well within the time given.

3. Grab the cards 抢卡片

准备材料 ➡ 活动页（见附页3.3）

方法 ➡ 教师将附页中的词语卡片剪下来，随意摆放在一张桌子中间，学生围在桌子旁边。教师说一个卡片上的词语，学生要迅速找到该词语并将卡片拿起，最后看谁抢到的词语卡片最多。

MATERIALS NEEDED ➡ Activity Page (See attachment 3.3)

METHOD ➡ The teacher cuts the word cards out of the Attachment Page, and then spreads the cards randomly in the middle of a desk. Have the students circle around the desk. The teacher then starts to say the words on the cards. The students are supposed to grab the card as quickly as they can and hold it up upon finding it. Compete to see which student grabs the most cards in the end.

4 They are so cool 他们真棒

A Let's learn 学一学

❶这部分学习由“真”构成的感叹句，基本格式是“主语+真+形容词”，例如“你真漂亮！”需要注意的是本课的句型“……真……”表示对人或事物的称赞，所以形容词一般是表示积极意义的词语，如“好、棒、可爱”等。“……真……”有时候也表示对人或事物的不满，这时使用的是表示消极意义的形容词，例如“笨、傻、懒”等。

❷教师利用本课的词语卡片，与学生一起练习句型。教师举起“漂亮”的卡片，用夸张的表情和语气说：“她真漂亮！”学生跟读。随后教师走到每个女学生的前面，微笑着说：“你真漂亮！”以此类推，练习本课学习的所有词语。“……真……”还可以扩展为“XX的……真……”，如“你的头发真漂亮！”

❸教师让学生打开书，看图，听录音，跟读课本中的句子。这部分配有替换词语，可以用来进行替换练习。练习之前教师把句型“……真……”写在黑板上，然后教师把课本举起来，指着替换部分的第一幅图做示范，说：“她真漂亮！”学生跟读。随后教师任意指一幅图，让学生说出句子。教师指图的速度可以越来越快，以此练习学生的反应

❶This section teaches the exclamatory sentence composed with “真(zhēn, really)”. Its basic structure is “subject + 真 + adjective”, for example, “你真漂亮！” It needs to be noticed that in this lesson “……真……” expresses the praise for the people or the things. Therefore, the adjectives used generally are those expressing the positivity, such as “好, 棒, 可爱”, etc. “……真……” sometimes also expresses the complaints. In these cases, the adjectives used are of the negative nature, such as “笨 (stupid), 傻 (silly), 懒 (lazy)”, etc.

❷The teacher uses the word cards in the lesson to practice the sentence patterns together with the students. The teacher raises the card with the word “漂亮”, using the exaggerated voice and tone to say: “她真漂亮！” The students then follow the teacher. After that, the teacher walks to every girl student in turn and says with a smile: “你真漂亮！” Continue the activity this way and have the students practice all the words in the lesson. “……真……” can be also expanded to “X X 的……真……” For example, “你的头发真漂亮！”

❸The teacher asks the students to open their books, look at the pictures, listen to the recording

第4课 他们真棒

tā men zhēn bàng

Let's learn 学一学 A

能力。

❹ 这部分内容学完后，教师可以用本课学习的句型对学生给予赞扬，一边鼓掌一边微笑着说：“你们真棒！”

and read after the sentences in the book. This section is provided with the substitute words, which can be used for the substitution exercise. Before the practice, the teacher writes down the sentence pattern “……真……” on the board, and then the teacher raises the book, points at the first picture with the substitute drills and says: “她真漂亮！” The students repeat after him. Then the teacher points at a picture randomly, and asks the students to say the sentences. The teacher may accelerate his speed at pointing at the pictures in order to train the students' reaction skills.

❹ After teaching this section, the teacher may use the sentence patterns taught in the lesson to praise the students, “你们真棒！” with smiles while clapping his hands.

TEXT TRANSLATION[课文译文]

他们真棒！ They are so cool!

B

PATTERN'S SUBSTITUTE[句型替换]

她/你真可爱！

它/猴子真聪明！

她/你真好！

她/你真漂亮！

他/你真帅！

Let's try 试一试

______ 真 ______ !
zhēn

kě'ài

cōngming

hǎo

piàoliang

shuài

A Look and sing 看一看，唱一唱

歌曲的学习方法参见本书的“使用说明”。

活动方法➡学生们学会歌曲以后，教师组织课堂活动：教师根据学生人数准备一些词语头饰，上边用拼音或者汉字分别写上“漂亮”、“帅”、“聪明”、“棒”、“好”。学生每人戴一个头饰，围成一圈，教师站在中间。教师指一个戴着“聪明”头饰的学生，大声说：“聪明”，然后教师打拍子，引导全班学生一起唱：“××真聪明。××真聪明。真聪明，真聪明……”以此类推，重复游戏，直到全班学生都得到练习。

歌曲文本➡丁丁真棒。丁丁真棒。棒棒棒棒棒棒。丁丁真棒。丁丁真棒。棒棒棒棒棒棒。美美真聪明。美美真聪明。真聪明。真聪明。美美真聪明。美美真聪明。真聪明，真聪明。

Refer to the *Teacher Manual* for the method for learning the song in the book.

ACTIVITY METHOD➡After the students have learned the song, the teacher organizes the class activity: the teacher prepares some headbands with the words or *pinyin* such as “漂亮”, “帅”, “聪明”, “棒” and “好” according to the students' number in the class. Each student puts one headband around his head and stands in a circle with the teacher in the middle. The teacher points at a student wearing the headband of “聪明” and says loudly: “聪明”. Then the teacher begins to beat time and lead the students in singing in chorus: “XX真聪明。XX真聪明。真聪明，真聪明……” Continue the activity till all the students have a chance to practice.

THE SONG SCRIPT➡Dingding is so cool. Dingding is so cool. Cool cool cool cool cool cool. Dingding is so cool. Dingding is so cool. Cool cool cool cool cool cool. Meimei is so smart. Meimei is so smart. So smart, so smart. Meimei is so smart. Meimei is so smart. So smart, so smart.

B Sentence patterns 学句型

Read the patterns aloud, and then look at the pictures and compose sentences with “真”. 大声朗读句型，然后看图用“真”完成句子。

❶ 这部分是句型总结与复习。教师先领学生反复大声朗读句型框里的句型，直到学生可以流利地读出句型框里的四个句子。

❶ This section is the summary of the sentence patterns and reviews. The teacher leads the students first in reading loud the sentence patterns in the box repeatedly till they can read out the four sentences in

4

Look and sing 看一看，唱一唱

A

Dīngdīng zhēn bàng.
Dīngdīng zhēn bàng.
Bàng bàng bàng bàng bàng bàng.
Dīngdīng zhēn bàng.
Dīngdīng zhēn bàng.
Bàng bàng bàng bàng bàng bàng.

Měimei zhēn cōngming.
Měimei zhēn cōngming.
Zhēn cōngming, zhēn cōngming.
Měimei zhēn cōngming.
Měimei zhēn cōngming.
Zhēn cōngming, zhēn cōngming.

28

Sentence patterns 学句型

B

- Read the patterns aloud, and then look at the pictures and complete the sentences with "真". 大声朗读句型，然后看图用"真"完成句子。

你 nǐ	真 zhēn	好 hǎo
你们 nǐmen		棒 bàng
妈妈 māma		漂亮 piàoliang
老师 lǎoshī		聪明 cōngming

Dàxiàng zhēn ________

Gǒu zhēn ________

Tā zhēn ________

Tā zhēn ________

4 They are so cool

29

Notes

❷ 学生看图，用句型“……真……”造句，可以用拼音或者汉字写出答案。本练习没有唯一的答案，学生可以发挥想象力，用本课学习的形容词完成句子。学生做完练习后，教师找学生分别读出自己写的句子。

the box fluently.

❷ The students look at the picture using sentence pattern “……真……” to make up sentences. They can also use *pinyin* or the characters to write out the answers. There is no one single correct answer in the exercise. The students can use their imagination to make up sentences with the adjectives learned in the lesson. After that the teacher chooses the students to read out their sentences they have written.

A Interesting characters 趣味汉字

本课学习的汉字是“儿”和“七”，要求学生掌握这两个字的正确写法。汉字的教学方法参见本书的“使用说明”。

This lesson teaches the characters “儿” and “七”. The students are required to master the correct way of writing these two characters. Refer to the *Teacher Manual* for the teaching method in the book.

B Let's do it 做一做

Listen to the teacher, and then quickly do the action. 听老师说，快速做出相应的动作。

方法 ➧ 按照学生用书第31页的要求做游戏。学生4~6人一组，站在教室前边。教师说“真大”或者“真小”，学生用手臂做出“大”或者“小”的动作。教师说词语的速度越来越快，学生的动作也要越来越快。做错的学生回到座位上，最后留下来的学生获胜。

活动扩展 ➧ 正说反做，即听到“真小”，学生要做出“大”的动作。

METHOD ➧ Start the game after the directions on page 31 on the Student's Book. Put 4-6 students in a group. They stand in the front of the class. The teacher says “真大” or “真小” while the students act out with their arms to respond with the corresponding moves. The teacher accelerates his utterances and the students react with faster pace accordingly. The student who makes a mistake goes back to his seat. The last remaining student wins in the end.

EXPANDED ACTIVITY ➧ Act out the opposite, i.e., at hearing “真小”, the students react with action showing “大”.

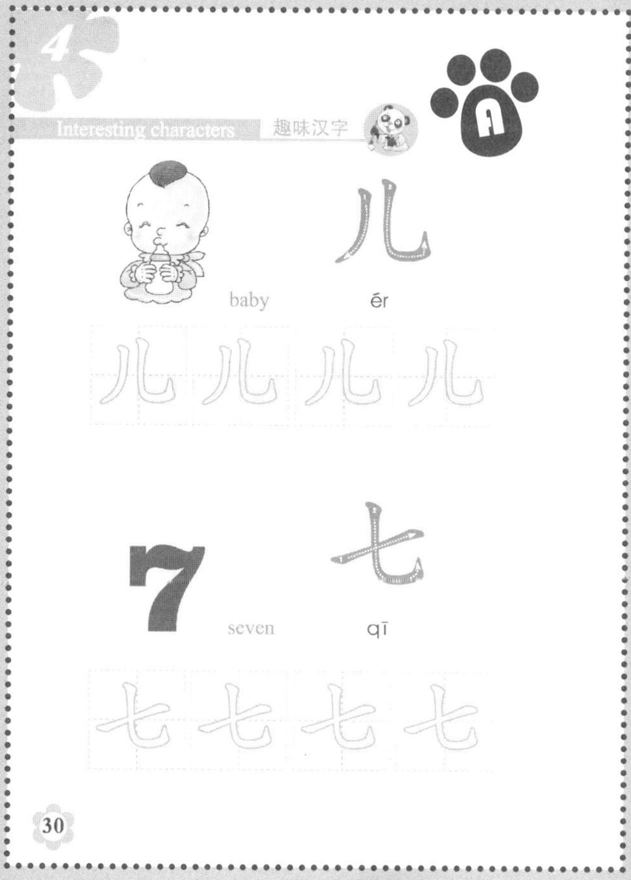

4

Interesting characters 趣味汉字

A

儿

baby ér

儿 儿 儿 儿

7 七

seven qī

七 七 七 七

30

Let's do it 做一做

B

- Listen to the teacher, and then quickly do the action. 听老师说，快速做出相应的动作。

4 They are so cool

31

Notes

Supplementary activities 补充活动

1. Arrange sentences with the characters 汉字拼句

准备材料 剪刀、活动页（见附页4.1）

方法 复印足够数量的活动页，发给每个学生一份。让学生把表格中的汉字和标点符号逐个剪下，拼出所给的四个句子，拼好后举手，教师走到学生身边，学生大声读出四个句子。

MATERIALS NEEDED scissors, Activity Page (See attachment 4.1)

METHOD Make enough copies of the Activity Page. Each student receives one copy. Have the students cut out the characters and the punctuation marks in the form and arrange out the four sentences given. When finished, the students raise their hands. The teacher then walks to the student who reads out the four sentences loud for the teacher.

2. Cut, paste and paint 剪一剪，粘一粘，涂一涂

准备材料 剪刀、胶棒、彩笔、活动页（见附页4.2）

方法 复印足够数量的活动页，发给每个学生一份。学生先把A图中的小图剪下来备用。教师说句子，如“大象的鼻子真长！”学生根据教师说的句子选择正确的小图，把它粘贴在B图相应的动物或人物的身上，然后用彩笔为B图涂上颜色。

参考句子

狗真可爱！

大象的鼻子真长！

鳄鱼的嘴巴真大！

她的衣服真漂亮！

MATERIALS NEEDED scissors, glue stick, color pens, Activity Page (See attachment 4.2)

METHOD Make enough copies of the Activity Page. Each student receives one copy. The students first cut out the small pictures in the picture A and store them for future use. The teacher says a sentence, for example, “大象的鼻子真长！” The students choose the correct small pictures according to the teacher's sentence, and then paste them onto the corresponding animals or the people in the picture B. Finally, have them paint the picture B with the color pens.

REFERENCE SENTENCES See the Chinese version on the left.

3. Whisper 悄悄话

方法 ➾ 将学生平均分为几组，每组4~6人，各站成一排。教师用本课所学的句型想好一个句子，如"××真帅！"教师轻声地把这个句子告诉每组的第一个学生，然后教师说"开始"，第一个学生把听到的句子轻声地传给第二个学生，这样依次传下去，最后一个学生把听到的句子说出来或者写在黑板上。所有小组都完成后，教师说出原句，看哪一组传得又好又快。

活动扩展 ➾ 教师也可以用拼音或者汉字把句子写在纸上，让每组的第一个学生看5~10秒钟，第一个学生把句子写下来再给第二个学生看5~10秒钟，这样依次传递到最后。教师把自己写的纸条和每组最后一名学生写的纸条粘贴在黑板上，让学生比较对错。

METHOD ➾ Divide the students into several groups. 4-6 people in a group. Each group stands in a line. The teacher uses the sentence pattern in the lesson to compose a sentence, for example, "××真帅！" Then the teacher whispers the sentence to the first student in the line. After that, the teacher says "开始". The first student starts to pass the sentence he has heard to the second student in the line in whisper. The second student then passes it to the third, so on and so forth. The last student either speaks it out or writes it out on the board. When done, the teacher speaks out the original sentence. Compete to see which group does it both quickly and accurately.

EXPANDED ACTIVITY ➾ The teacher can also write out the sentence in *pinyin* or the characters on the paper and asks the first student in each group to read it in 5-10 seconds. The first student then writes it down and shows it to the second student for 5-10 seconds. Continue the game like this till it reaches the last students in the lines. Both the teacher and the last student in each group paste the sentence on the board, and let the students see which group is right and which is wrong.

REVIEW 2 复习

A Look, write and say 看一看，写一写，说一说

准备材料 ▶▶ 要求学生准备一张本人的照片、胶棒、剪刀

方法 ▶▶ 按照学生用书第32页的要求做练习。学生根据图画用拼音或者汉字完成句子。这部分没有唯一的答案，学生可以自行发挥。最后一个题目需要学生将自己的照片粘贴到课本上，并且完成句子。学生们做练习时，教师在教室巡视，给予个别指导。最后，教师组织全班活动，即教师任意说一个本课学习的词语或者句子，如“可爱”或者“她真可爱！”学生们在自己的课本上指出相应的图片。

MATERIALS NEEDED ▶▶ Have each student prepare a photo of him, glue stick, and scissors

METHOD ▶▶ Have the students do the exercises after the directions on page 32 in the Student Book. The students use either *pinyin* or the characters to finish up the sentences according to the pictures. This section has no single correct answer. The students can use their imagination to create their own answers. The last topic is for the students to paste their photos onto the books, and finish up the sentences. While the students are working on their exercises the teacher walks around among the students providing assistance on the individual basis. Lastly, the teacher organizes the whole class activity, i.e., the teacher says a sentence or a word taught in the lesson, for example, “可爱” or “她真可爱！” while the students point out the corresponding picture on their books.

B Story time 故事会

教学方法参见本书的“使用说明”。

故事文本 ▶▶ 美美和兰兰在路边看到一个男生，他长得很帅，穿得很时髦。他正在一边吃香蕉一边听音乐。兰兰说：“他真帅！”男生吃完了香蕉，随手就把香蕉皮扔在了地上。美美很吃惊：“啊？”美美和兰兰都不喜欢这个男生了，因为他很没有礼貌。这时候，一个长相很普通的男生走了过来，捡起香蕉皮，扔进垃圾桶里。美美和兰兰很喜欢

Refer to the *Teacher Manual* for the teaching method in the book.

STORY TEXT ▶▶ Meimei and Lanlan saw a boy on the roadside. He was very handsome and dressed fashionably. He was eating a banana while listening to the music. Lanlan said: “他真帅！” After he finished up the banana he dropped the peel on the ground conveniently. Meimei was surprised: “啊？” Then both Meimei and Lanlan lost their

Review 2 (复习2)

A

1 Look, write and say 看一看，写一写，说一说

Tā zhēn ________!

Tā zhēn ________!

Tā zhēn ________!

Tā zhēn ________!

Tā zhēn ________!

my photo

Wǒ zhēn ________!

32

2 Story time 故事会

B

33

Notes

这个男生，美美说：“他真好！”

favorite impression of the boy because he didn't know how to behave in the public places. Just at this time, a very ordinary looking boy came over and picked up the peel and threw it into the trash can. Meimei and Lanlan were very fond of the boy. Meimei said: “他真好！”

TRANSLATION[译文] 图1：他真帅！He is so handsome!
图2：啊？Ah?
图3：他真好！He is so kind!

Unit Three 第三单元

第五课： 日期
第六课： 今天五月八号

教学目标：
Objectives
❶ 拼音：g k h
❷ 句型：今天……月……号，星期……

生词：
New Words
昨天・今天・明天・月・号・星期・星期天

语言点：
Language Point
表示日期的名词谓语句

日常用语：
Daily Expressions
❶ A：你几点上学？ B：我九点上学。
❷ A：你几点放学？ B：我三点放学。

汉字：
Chinese Characters
九 几

活动：
Activity
制作月历

Introduction 导入

❶ 教师准备几张与“漂亮”、“帅”、“聪明”、“棒”有关的图片，如人物、动物、中国功夫、体育比赛等，引导学生用“……真……”表达对人物或者动物的赞美，随后教师领读正确的句子，学生跟读。以此复习前一单元学习的内容。

❷ 教师带领学生复习数字，能够流利地从1数到50。然后教师在黑板上用从上到下的顺序依次写出数字1~12，让学生大声读出来。随后教师在数字后边写上“月”或者贴上“月”的词语卡片，领读“一月”到“十二月”。用这种方法依次学习“×号”和“星期×”。

❸ 教师提前准备好一张当月的月历，上边写有日期和星期。教师把月历贴在黑板上，让学生找到当天的日期，然后教师领读：“今天×月×号，星期×”，“昨天×月×号，星期×”，“明天×月×号，星期×”，直到学生能熟练地说出这三个句子。

❶ The teacher prepares a few pictures related to the words “漂亮”, “帅”, “聪明” and “棒”. These pictures can be about people, animals, Chinese Martial Art, and sports competitions. The teacher uses these visual aides to guide the students in using “……真……” expressing the praise for the people or the animals. The teacher then leads in reading the correct sentences and asks the students to follow him so that the former unit gets reviewed.

❷ First, the teacher leads the students in reviewing the numbers. The students should be able to count from 1-50 fluently. The teacher then writes down vertically the numbers 1-12 on the board. Have the students read them out loud. Next, the teacher writes “月” or pastes the word card of it next to the numbers. Lead in reading the names of the months from “一月” to “十二月”. Use this way to teach “×号” and “星期×” in turn.

❸ The teacher brings in a current monthly calendar prepared before the class. It has the dates and weekdays on it. Then hang it on the board. Have the students find today's date and then lead in reading: “今天×月×号，星期×”, “昨天×月×号，星期×”, “明天×月×号，星期×”, till the students can say the three sentences fluently.

Notes

第5课 日期
rì qī
Let's read 读一读
Gg guō
Kk kūn
Hh huā
34

Notes

5 Date 日期

Let's read 读一读

❶学习声母g、k、h的读音。
❷学习g、k、h与韵母的拼合。

❶ Learn the pronunciations of the initials g, k, h.
❷ Learn the combination of the initials g, k, h and the finals.

A Exercise 练一练

Listen and mark the tones. 听录音，标声调。

☀ KEY··答案

gē	gé	gě	gè
kē	ké	kě	kè
hē	hé	hě	hè

B Activity 课堂活动

One student raises a *pinyin* card, and the other two students quickly find the *pinyin* letter on the board. Let's see who can find it first. 一个小朋友举拼音卡片，另外两个小朋友在黑板上快速找出卡片上的那个拼音，看谁先找到。

准备材料 ▶▶ 一些包含有g、k、h的词语卡片，以及声母g、k、h的拼音卡片。

方法 ▶▶ 按照学生用书第35页的要求做游戏。教师将词语卡片粘贴在黑板上，把拼音卡片g、k、h分发给三个学生，然后找另外两个学生到黑板前指认卡片。教师说："1－2－3，开始！"拿着拼音卡片的学生要快速举起自己手中的卡片，并读出卡片上的拼音，如"g"，先举起卡片并正确读出拼音的学生获胜，其他两个学生则要把卡片放下。随后，黑板前的两个学生要快速在黑板上找出包含有"g"的词卡，指出来，并大声读出词语。先找到卡片并正确读出词语的学生留在前边，继续跟下一个学生比赛，直到全班学生都得到练习。教师可以根据情况随时更换持有拼音卡片的学生，以及黑板上词语卡片的位置。

活动扩展 ▶▶ 在规定的时间内，让学生在黑板上的词语卡片中找出一共有几

MATERIALS NEEDED ▶▶ Prepare some word cards containing g, k, and h, as well as the *pinyin* cards with g, k, and h as the initials.

METHOD ▶▶ Start the game after the directions on page 35 in the Student Book. The teacher pastes the word cards on the board and gives the *pinyin* cards containing g, k, and h to three students. Then find other two students and ask them to come to the front to identify the cards. The teacher says: "1－2－3，开始！ (one-two-three, start!)" The student holding the *pinyin* cards should raise their cards immediately, and read the *pinyin* on the cards. For example, "g". The student who raises the card first and reads out its *pinyin* correctly wins. The other two students should put down their cards. After that, the two students up in the front should find the cards with "g" quickly and read it out loud. The student who first finds the letter and reads it out correctly remains in the front to con-

Exercise 练一练 A

- Listen and mark the tones. 听录音，标声调。

ge	ge	ge	ge
ke	ke	ke	ke
he	he	he	he

Activity 课堂活动 B

- One student raises a *pinyin* card, and the other two students quickly find the *pinyin* letter on the board. Let's see who can find it first. 一个小朋友举拼音卡片，另外两个小朋友在黑板上快速找出卡片上的那个拼音，看谁先找到。

个g，几个k，几个h，看谁找得又快又好。

tinue the game with the next student. The game goes on like this till all the students get a chance to practice. The teacher can replace the students holding the cards at any time according to the situation as well as change the card positions on the board.

EXPANDED ACTIVITY Have the students find how many g, k, and h in total respectively on the word cards on the board in the time given. Compete to see who finishes both fast and best.

A Let's recognize 认一认

这部分是本课学习的词语，教学方法参见本书的“使用说明”。

This section teaches the words in the lesson. Refer to the *Teacher Manual* for the teaching method in the book.

教学建议：可以运用“时间轴”帮助学生学习“×天”，如：

Teaching suggestion: the “time axle” below can be used to help the students learning “X day”, for example:

大前天　前天　昨天　今天　明天　后天　大后天

SUPPLEMENTARY WORDS[补充生词]

后天 the day after tomorrow
hòutiān

大后天 the day after the day of tomorrow
dàhòutiān

前天 the day before yesterday
qiántiān

大前天 the day before the day of yesterday
dàqiántiān

星期日 Sunday
Xīngqīrì

B Exercises 练一练

1. Listen and write. 听录音，写汉字。

KEY · · 答案

星期 一　星期 二　星期 三

星期 四　星期 五　星期 六

录音文本：
星期一，星期二
星期三，星期四
星期五，星期六

2. Look and fill in the blanks. 看一看，填一填。

KEY · · 答案

星期天 Xīngqītiān	星期一 Xīngqīyī	星期二 Xīngqī'èr	星期三 Xīngqīsān	星期四 Xīngqīsì	星期五 Xīngqīwǔ	星期六 Xīngqīliù
5月5号	5月6号	5月7号	5月8号	5月9号	5月10号	5月11号

5

Let's recognize 认一认

A

昨天 zuótiān yesterday	今天 jīntiān today	明天 míngtiān tomorrow
月 yuè month	号 hào date	星期 xīngqī week

星期一	Xīngqīyī	Monday
星期二	Xīngqī'èr	Tuesday
星期三	Xīngqīsān	Wednesday
星期四	Xīngqīsì	Thursday
星期五	Xīngqīwǔ	Friday
星期六	Xīngqīliù	Saturday
星期天	Xīngqītiān	Sunday

36

B

Exercises 练一练

1 Listen and write. 听录音，写汉字。

星期 ○　星期 ○　星期 ○

星期 ○　星期 ○　星期 ○

5 Date

2 Look and fill in the blanks. 看一看，填一填。

星期天	星期___	星期二	星期___	___四	星期___	___六
___	Xīngqī___	Xīngqī'èr	Xīngqī___	___sì	Xīngqī___	___liù

5月6号　　5月11号

37

Notes

Activity 课堂活动

While looking at the date on the board, the teacher says a date. Listen and decide what day of the week it is. 看一看黑板上的日期，再听老师说一个日期，想一想老师说的日期是星期几。

方法 ▶▶ 教师在黑板上写下一个日期，如"六月三号，星期三"，然后说一个临近的日期，如"六月四号"，让学生根据黑板上的日期抢答"六月四号"是星期几，也可找学生说一个临近的日期，其他学生猜猜是星期几。

活动扩展 ▶▶ 教师可以加上"今天"、"昨天"、"明天"等词语，例如在黑板上写"今天六月三号，星期三"，让学生抢答昨天和明天的日期。

METHOD ▶▶ The teacher writes out a date on the board, for example, "六月三号，星期三" and then says a date next to it, for example, "六月四号". Then have the students compete to answer which weekday the June 4 is based on the information on the board, or choose a student to say a date close to today's date and have other students guess its weekday.

EXPANDED ACTIVITY ▶▶ The teacher can add the words like "今天", "昨天" or "明天", for example, write "今天六月三号，星期三" on the board and let the students compete to answer yesterday's and tomorrow's dates.

Let's say 说一说

教学方法参见本书的"使用说明"。

词语替换 ▶▶ 课本对话中表示时间的"×点"可以替换。

Refer to the *Teacher Manual* for the teaching method in the book.

WORDS SUBSTITUTION ▶▶ "×点" expressing time in the dialogue can be substituted.

5

Activity 课堂活动

A

- While looking at the date on the board, the teacher says a date. Listen and decide what day of the week it is. 看一看黑板上的日期，再听老师说一个日期，想一想老师说的日期是星期几。

38

Let's say 说一说

B

5 Date

39

Notes

Supplementary activities 补充活动

1. Look for stars 找星星

准备材料 彩笔、活动页（见附页5.1）

方法 复印足够数量的活动页，发给每个学生一份。教师在每行三个拼音里随意找一个读出来，学生用彩笔把写有该拼音的星星涂上自己喜欢的颜色。涂好后每个学生分别读一遍自己的答案。完全涂对的学生可以得到一个小奖励。

MATERIALS NEEDED color pens, Activity Page (See attachment 5.1)

METHOD Make enough copies of the Activity Page. Each student receives one copy. The teacher picks one *pinyin* among the three on each line and reads it out. The students use the color pens to paint the star which has the sound with their favorite colors. After that, the students read out their findings in turn. The students who have done the task perfectly may get a small prize.

2. Arrange and write out the *pinyin* 排一排，写拼音

准备材料 活动页（见附页5.2）

方法 复印足够数量的活动页，发给每个学生一份。学生根据所给的汉字，把正确的拼音排列出来，写在汉字的旁边。写好后，教师把活动页收上来，给出评价。

MATERIALS NEEDED the Activity Page (See attachment 5.2)

METHOD Make enough copies of the Activity Page. Each student receives one copy. The students spell out the correct *pinyin* based on the characters provided, and write them out next to the characters. The teacher then collects them and gives feedback.

3. Look for dates 找日期

准备材料 两本当年的挂历或者台历

方法 将学生分为两组，每组选一名组长，发一本挂历或者台历。第一组组长选一个学生说出自己的生日是几月几号（可以不说哪一年），第二组组长派一个学生在30秒以内找出那一天是星期

MATERIALS NEEDED Two current hanging or desktop calendars

METHOD Divide the students into two groups. Each group elects one leader, and receives one calendar, either hanging or desktop. The first group leader chooses one student to say his birthday (the year can be

儿，并报告给大家。正确的加1分，错误的不加分。教师负责计时、计分。接下来，第二组负责报告的学生说出自己的生日是几月几号，第一组组长再派一个学生找出那一天是星期几。以此类推，直到所有学生都得到练习。活动中，各组可以派一个学生记住每个人的生日都是星期几，最后统计一下当年星期几过生日的人最多。

示例 1.（我的生日是）三月五号。

2. 三月五号，星期六。

omitted). The second group leader designates one student to find the weekday of that birthday in 30 seconds and reports to the class. If his answer is correct he gets one point; if wrong he gets a zero point. The teacher is in charge of keeping the time and the points. Then the student in the second group who has reported the weekday speaks out his birthday. The first group leader then designates a teammate from his group to find the weekday of the birthday said. Continue the game this way till all the students get a chance to practice. During this activity, each group can choose one student to remember the weekdays of each student. Lastly, calculate and compare which weekday happens to be the most students' birthday.

EXAMPLE See the Chinese version on the left.

Today is May 8th 今天五月八号

Let's learn 学一学

❶ 这部分学习名词谓语句。名词谓语句中的谓语不是由动词充当，而是直接由名词或名词性短语充当，通常用来表示日期、年龄等。表示日期的名词谓语句的基本格式是“今天/明天/昨天×月×号，星期×”，例如“明天六月一号，星期二”。

❷ 教师指着日历，用疑惑的表情和语气询问学生：“今天几月几号？”“今天星期几？”学生用汉语回答：“今天×月×号”，“今天星期×”。教师对学生的帮助表示感谢，随后把两个句子合起来说：“哦！今天×月×号，星期×。”教师再重复问几次日期，让学生一起回答。随后教师把“今天”换成“明天”和“昨天”，这两个词在语气上要重一些，以引起学生的注意，同时引导学生回答“明天×月×号，星期×”，“昨天×月×号，星期×”。

❸ 教师让学生打开书，一边看图一边听录音，跟读课本中的句子。随后让学生自己把另外两句话补充完整。最后做一个替换练习的小游戏：教师在课本上任指一个日期，让学生说出句子：“今天×月×号，星期×”；也可以把学生分为两人一组，一人指日期，另一人说句子。

❶ This section teaches the noun predicate sentence which can't be made by a verb. It can be made only by a noun or a noun phrase. It is usually used to express date or age, etc. The basic structure of a noun predicate sentence expressing date goes like this: “今天/明天/昨天×月×号，星期×”, for example, “明天六月一号，星期二”.

❷ The teacher points at the calendar and asks the students in a confused facial expression and tone: “今天星期几？(What is the date today?)” The students then answer in Chinese: “今天×月×号”, “今天星期×”. The teacher then expresses appreciation for the students' help, puts the two sentences together and says: “哦！今天×月×号，星期×。” The teacher then repeats the question a couple of times and have the students respond in chorus. After that, the teacher changes “今天” into “明天” and “昨天”. Stress these two words so to get the students' attention. Guide the students in answering “明天×月×号，星期×”, “昨天×月×号，星期×”.

❸ The teacher asks the students to open their books, look at the pictures, listen to the recording and follow the reading of the sentences in the lesson. Then have the students complete the other two sen-

第6课 今天五月八号

jīn tiān wǔ yuè bā hào

Let's learn 学一学

40

tences. Lastly, the teacher may start a little substitute game: the teacher points at a picture in the lesson randomly and have the students say the sentence: "今天×月×号，星期×". The teacher may also divide the students into two groups, one student points at the date and the other says a sentence.

TEXT TRANSLATION[课文译文]

今天五月八号，星期二。Today is May 8th, Tuesday.

Thursday 四	Friday 五	Saturday 六
3 十七	4 十八	5 十九
10 廿四	11 廿五	12 廿六
17 四月	18 初二	19 初三
24 初八	25 初九	26 初十
31 十五		

A Sing and play a game 唱一唱，做接龙游戏

歌曲的学习方法参见本书的“使用说明”。

活动方法➜学生们学会歌曲以后，教师组织课堂活动：把“星期一”到“星期天”的七张词语卡片散放在一张桌子上，三个学生一组，站在桌子旁边。教师指其中一个学生，说“开始”，被指的学生任选一张卡片，如“星期三”，然后开始唱歌：“星期三呀，星期三呀，今天今天星期三”；教师接着指另外一个学生，被指的学生要快速拿起“星期二”的卡片，接着唱“昨天昨天星期二呀”，教师再指第三个学生，被指的学生快速拿起“星期四”的卡片，接着唱“明天明天星期四”。这个活动也可以将全班学生分为三个小组，组与组之间进行歌曲接龙游戏。

歌曲文本➜星期五呀，星期五呀。今天今天星期五。昨天昨天星期四呀。明天明天星期六。

Refer to the *Teacher Manual* for the method for learning the song in the book.

ACTIVITY METHOD➜After the students have learned the song, the teacher organizes the class activity: spread the word cards with “星期一” to “星期天” on one desktop. Three students are put in a group, standing around the desk. The teacher points at one of the students and says: “开始”. The student being pointed at chooses one card at will, for example, “星期三”, then starts to sing “星期三呀，星期三呀，今天今天星期三”. The teacher then points at another student who is supposed to pick up the “星期二” card quickly, and then continues to sing “昨天昨天星期二呀”. The teacher points at the third student who quickly picks up the “星期四” card and goes on to sing “明天明天星期四”. This activity also can be done with the students divided into three groups, which conduct the song connection game among themselves.

THE SONG SCRIPT➜Friday. Friday. Today today is Friday. Yesterday yesterday was Thursday. Tomorrow tomorrow is Saturday.

B Sentence patterns 学句型

Read the patterns aloud, and then complete the following two sentences according to the example sentence. 大声朗读句型，然后根据所给例句完成其他两个句子。

❶ 这部分是句型总结与复习。教师先领学生反复大声朗读句型框里的句型，

❶ This section is the summary of the sentence patterns and reviews. The teacher first leads the students

6

A

Sing and play a game 唱一唱，做接龙游戏

Xīngqīwǔ ya.

Xīngqīwǔ ya.

Jīntiān jīntiān Xīngqīwǔ.

Zuótiān zuótiān Xīngqīsì ya.

Míngtiān míngtiān Xīngqīliù.

42

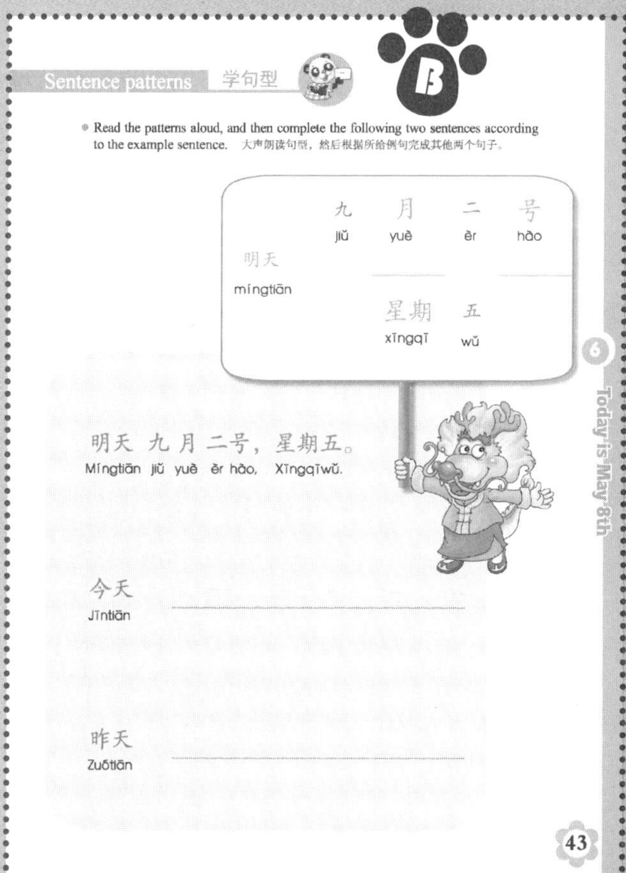

B

Sentence patterns 学句型

- Read the patterns aloud, and then complete the following two sentences according to the example sentence. 大声朗读句型，然后根据所给例句完成其他两个句子。

	九 jiǔ	月 yuè	二 èr	号 hào
明天 míngtiān		星期 xīngqī	五 wǔ	

明天 九 月 二号，星期五。
Míngtiān jiǔ yuè èr hào, Xīngqīwǔ.

今天
Jīntiān ____________________

昨天
Zuótiān ____________________

6 Today is May 8th

43

Notes

直到学生可以流利地读出句型框里的两个句子。

❷ 学生根据所给句子完成其他两个句子，可以用拼音或者汉字写出答案，教师个别指导。学生做完练习后，教师找学生分别把自己写的答案读出来。

in reading out the sentence patterns in the box repeatedly and loudly till the students can read the two sentences in the box fluently.

❷ The students finish up the other two sentences based on the sentences given. They can use the *pinyin* or the characters to write out the answers while the teacher supervises individually. After the practice, the teacher asks the students to read out their answers respectively.

KEY · · 答案

今天九月一号，星期四。　昨天八月三十一号，星期三。

A Interesting characters 趣味汉字

本课学习的汉字是“九”和“儿”，要求学生掌握这两个字的正确写法。汉字的教学方法参见本书的“使用说明”。

This lesson teaches the characters “九” and “儿”. The students are required to master the correct way of writing these two characters. Refer to the *Teacher Manual* for the teaching method in the book.

B Let's do it 做一做

Make a calender of the current month, and then circle the days you like. 做一张本月的月历，并圈出你最喜欢的日子。

准备材料 ➡ 铅笔、彩笔

方法 ➡ 按照学生用书第45页的图示，让学生在表格里填写出日期和星期。填写完成后，学生可以用彩笔装饰一下月历，然后圈出自己最喜欢的日子。教师让学生用汉语说出喜欢哪些日子，用英语说出喜欢的原因。

MATERIALS NEEDED ➡ pencils, color pencils

METHOD ➡ Have the students fill in the dates and weekdays on the monthly chart after the illustrations on page 45 in the Student Book. After that, the students can decorate the calendar with the color pencils, and then circle out their most favorite days. Lastly, the teacher asks the students to say which days they like most in Chinese and give the reasons in English.

6

A

Interesting characters 趣味汉字

9 nine 九 jiǔ

九 九 九 九

how many 几 jǐ

几 几 几 几

B

Let's do it 做一做

- Make a calender of the current month, and then circle the days you like.
  做一张本月的月历，并圈出你最喜欢的日子。

星期日	星期一	星期二	星期三	星期四	星期五	星期六

6 Today is May 8th

Notes

Supplementary activities 补充活动

1. Match the sentences 句子配对

准备材料▶剪刀、活动页（见附页6.1）

方法▶学生两人一组，复印活动页，发给每组一份。学生先将表格中的句子剪下来，然后找出中英文意思相同的句子，把它们拼在一起。完成后举手，其中一人读英文句子，另一人读出相应的中文句子。

MATERIALS NEEDED▶scissors, Activity Page (See attachment 6.1)

METHOD▶Put two students in a group. Make copies of the Activity Page. Each group receives a copy. The students first cut out the sentences, and then find the sentences with the same meaning. After done, the student raises his hand to get the teacher's attention. One student reads out the English sentence, the other reads out the corresponding Chinese sentence.

2. Look for the festivals 找节日

准备材料▶根据学生人数，准备足够数量的挂历。

方法▶学生两人一组，发给每组一本当年的挂历。教师用汉语和英语说出某个节日的名称，学生在挂历上找出相应的日期，然后抢答"×月×号，星期×"。回答正确1分，回答错误扣1分。教师负责计分。

活动扩展▶将全班学生分成两大组，每组发一本挂历。每组学生用汉语或者英语写出尽可能多的节日名称，然后轮流派一个组员问对方小组这些节日的时间，对方要在30秒内回答出"×月×号，星期×"。回答正确加1分，超时或者回答错误扣1分。教师负责计分。活动结束后，可以把找到的节日写出来，做一个漂亮的节日表，挂在教室的墙上，在每个节日的当天一起庆祝。

MATERIALS NEEDED▶Prepare enough calendars according to the number of the students.

METHOD▶Put two students into a group. Each group receives a current calendar. The teacher says a name of a festival in both Chinese and English; the students then start to look for the corresponding festival on their calendars, and then compete to answer "×月×号，星期×". The correct answer gets one point; the wrong one gets one point deducted. The teacher is in charge of keeping the points.

EXPANDED ACTIVITY▶Divide the students into two big groups. Each group receives one calendar. Each group tries to write out as many as festival names as they can in Chinese or English, and then have one group member ask the other group about the dates of these festivals.

The other group will do the same to the opposing group. The response time is thirty seconds. The answer has to be "×月×号，星期×". The correct answer gets one point; the wrong one gets one point deducted. The teacher is in charge of keeping the scores. At the end of the activity, the students can make a beautiful chart of the festivals and hang it on the wall in the classroom. Celebrate the festival when it comes.

参考节日　Festivals for reference

中国的节日	西方的节日
元旦 Yuándàn New Year's Day 1月1日	新年 Xīnnián New Year's Day 1月1日
除夕 Chúxī New Year's Eve 腊月的最后一天	情人节 Qíngrén Jié Valentine's Day 2月14日
春节 Chūn Jié Spring Festival 农历正月初一	复活节 Fùhuó Jié Easter 春分后月圆后的第一个星期日（3月21日~4月25日）
元宵节 Yuánxiāo Jié Lantern Festival 农历正月十五	愚人节 Yúrén Jié April Fool's Day 4月1日
劳动节 Láodòng Jié Labour Day 5月1日	母亲节 Mǔqīn Jié Mother's Day 5月的第二个星期日
端午节 Duānwǔ Jié Dragon Boat Festival 农历五月初五	父亲节 Fùqīn Jié Father's Day 6月的第三个星期日
儿童节 Értóng Jié Children's Day 6月1日	万圣节 Wànshèng Jié Hallowmas 11月1日
中秋节 Zhōngqiū Jié Moon Festival 农历八月十五	感恩节 Gǎn'ēn Jié Thanksgiving Day 11月第四个星期四
教师节 Jiàoshī Jié Teacher's Day 9月10日	平安夜 Píng'ānyè Christmas Eve 12月24日
国庆节 Guóqìng Jié National Day 10月1日	圣诞节 Shèngdàn Jié Christmas Day 12月25日

3. Think and write down the dates　想一想，写日期

准备材料 ▶▶ 活动页（见附页6.3）

方法 ▶▶ 复印足够数量的活动页，发给每个学生一份，让学生将日历填写完整。完成后，教师组织全班活动：教师说出这个月第一天的日期，如"6月1号"，其他学生依次数下去，从第一天一直数到最后一天。也可以教师说"星期×"，学生举手抢答日期，如教师说"星期一"，学生说"6月7号"、"6月14号"、"6月21号"、"6月28号"。

MATERIALS NEEDED ▶▶ Activity Page (See attachment 6.3)

METHOD ▶▶ Make enough copies of the Activity Page. Give each student a copy. Have the students fill out the dates and then the teacher starts to organize the whole class activity: the teacher says the first day of the month, for example, "6月1号", the students take it over and continue the counting, from the first day till the last one. It also can be done with the teacher saying the weekdays and the students compete to answer the dates, for example, the teacher says "星期一", the students then say "6月7号", "6月14号", "6月21号" and "6月28号".

REVIEW 3 复习

A Find, write and say 找一找，写一写，说一说

Using the cards beld in the hands of the same animals, compose three sentences.
找出同一种动物，用它们手中的词语造三个句子，并写出来。

方法 学生看图，用动物手中的词语造句，例如："昨天三月三号，星期一"。可以用拼音或者汉字把句子写出来。写完后，教师说一个提示词，如"昨天"，学生们一起说出句子："昨天三月三号，星期一"。

METHOD The students look at the pictures, using the words in the animals' hands to make up sentences. For example: "昨天三月三号，星期一", which can be written out in either *pinyin* or the characters. After that, the teacher says a cue word, for example, "昨天"; the students then speak out the sentence: "昨天三月三号，星期一".

KEY · 答案

昨天三月三号，星期一。今天三月四号，星期二。明天三月五号，星期三。

B Story time 故事会

教学方法参见本书的"使用说明"。

故事文本 丁丁早上起床时，看到日历上的日期是九月五号。九月五号是他的生日！丁丁高兴地跑到厨房告诉妈妈："今天九月五号。"妈妈正在做早饭，没有说话。丁丁又跑到花园里告诉爸爸："今天九月五号。"爸爸正在打太极拳，也没有说话。丁丁很难过，爸爸妈妈都不记得他的生日了。他失望地跟爸爸说："再见。"然后就去上学了。下午丁丁放学回到家里，一进家门就看到一个大大的生日蛋糕，爸爸和妈妈高兴地对他说："生日快乐！"原来爸爸妈妈是想给他一个惊喜。丁丁真高兴！

Refer to the *Teacher Manual* for the teaching method in the book.

STORY TEXT When Dingding got out off his bed in the morning he saw today was September 5th, his birthday! He ran into the kitchen and told his mom: "今天九月五号。" Since Mom was busy cooking, she didn't say anything. Dingding then ran into the garden and told his Dad: "今天九月五号。" Since his Dad was playing the *Shadow Boxing*, he didn't say anything, either. Dingding felt very sad, because both his Mom and Dad didn't remember his birthday. He said to his Dad disappointedly: "再见。" and then went to school. When Dingding

Review 3（复习3）

A

1 Find, write and say 找一找，写一写，说一说

- Using the cards held in the hands of the same animals, compose three sentences.
  找出同一种动物，用它们手中的词语造三个句子，并写出来。

______ ______ 月 ______ 号，星期 ______。

1. ______________，______________。
2. ______________，______________。
3. ______________，______________。

46

B

2 Story time 故事会

47

Notes

came back home from the school in the afternoon he saw a big birthday cake as soon as he entered the door. Mom and Dad both said happily: “生日快乐！” It turned out that Dingding’s parents wanted to give him a pleasant surprise. Dingding was really happy!

TRANSLATION[译文] 图2：今天九月五号。Today is September 5th.

图3：今天九月五号。Today is September 5th.

图4：再见！Bye.

图5：生日快乐！Happy birthday!

Unit Four 第四单元

第七课： 水果
第八课： 我吃苹果

教学目标：
Objectives
❶ 拼音：j q x
❷ 句型：……吃/喝……

生词：
New Words
吃 · 香蕉 · 苹果 · 菠萝 · 葡萄 · 草莓 · 喝 · 水 · 茶

语言点：
Language Point
由“吃/喝”构成的动词谓语句

日常用语：
Daily Expressions
❶ A：老师，我想去洗手间，可以吗？
B：可以。
❷ A：请问，洗手间在哪里？
B：在那里。

汉字：
Chinese Characters
门 月

活动：
Activity
制作招贴画

Introduction 导入

❶ 教师准备好1~31的数字卡片，其中1~12的卡片需要准备两套；另外还要准备“今天”、“昨天”、“明天”、“月”、“号”，以及“星期一”到“星期天”的词语卡片。教师把卡片散放在教室前边的一张桌子上，然后找六个学生站在桌子旁边。教师说一个表示日期的句子，如“今天6月25号，星期一”。六个学生要快速在桌子上找出相应的卡片并拿起来，然后按正确的顺序站成一排，排成句子“今天6月25号，星期一”。站好后每个人先按顺序读出自己卡片上的词语，然后一起读出整个句子。重复这个游戏，直到全班同学都得到练习。游戏做完后，教师询问学生：“今天几月几号？星期几？”“昨天呢？”“明天呢？”学生回答后，教师利用卡片重复答案，学生跟读。以此复习前一个单元学习的内容。

❷ 教师准备几种当地常见的水果，如香蕉、苹果、菠萝、葡萄、草莓等。如果没有水果，也可以使用本课的词语卡片。先让学生看实物或卡片，用英语或者汉语说出水果的名称，然后教师领读，学生跟读；随后教师走到学生中间，用汉语说出水果名称，让学生指出相应的实物或者卡片。以此引入本课学习的内容。

❶ The teacher prepares the number cards 1-31. Two sets of cards for the numbers 1-12. He also needs to prepare the word cards for “今天”, “昨天”, “明天”, “月”, “号” as well as the cards from “星期一” to “星期天”. The teacher spreads the cards on the desktop in front of the classroom, and then asks six students to come to stand alongside of the desk. The teacher starts to say a sentence expressing the date, for example, “今天6月25号，星期一”. The six students should look for and take the corresponding cards on the desktop as soon as possible. After that they stand in the correct sequence to make a sentence: “今天6月25号，星期一”. After that, each student reads out the word on his card according to his position. Lastly the students read out the complete sentence together. Repeat the game till all the students in the class get a chance to practice. After the game, the teacher asks the students: “今天几月几号，星期几？”“昨天呢？”“明天呢？” After the students have answered the questions, the teacher uses the cards to repeat the answers and have the students read after him so as to review the previous Unit.

❷ The teacher prepares a few kinds of the local fruits, such as banana, apple, grapes, and strawberry. If that’s impossible, the teacher can also prepare the word cards in the lesson. First, have the students see the real objects or the cards and speak out the names of the fruits in either English or Chinese, and then the teacher leads the students in reading out the names of the fruits. The students read after the teacher. Then the teacher walks around the students saying the names of the fruits in Chinese and have the students point at the corresponding real objects or the cards so to introduce the students to the content to be taught in the lesson.

Notes

Fruits 水果 7

Let's read 读一读

❶ 学习声母j、q、x的读音。

❷ 学习j、q、x与韵母的拼合。

❶ Learn the pronunciations of the initials j, q, and x.

❷ Learn the combination of the initials j, q, x and the finals.

A Exercise 练一练

Listen and mark the tones. 听录音，标声调。

KEY · · 答案

jiā quǎn xiǎng qiè xué qín xìng jiǔ jūn qióng

B Activity 课堂活动

With three to six students in a group, find the *pinyin* cards and place them under the flash cards to make a word. 三到六个小朋友一组，把找到的拼音卡片贴在相应的图片下边，拼成一个词语。

准备材料 两套拼音卡片（包括声调卡片）、一些包含有拼音 j、q、x 的词语卡片

方法 将学生分为两组，每组分一套拼音卡片。教师将词语卡片贴在黑板上，按照学生用书第49页的图示做游戏。教师任指一张词语卡片，学生要根据词卡上的拼音快速找到相应的拼音卡片，然后拿着拼音卡片跑到教室前边，按照正确的顺序排成一行，把拼音卡片举起来，拼成词语卡片上的词语，并一起大声读出拼音。最先找到卡片并且正确拼出词语的小组加1分，拼错的不加分。教师负责计分。重复这个游戏，直到黑板上的词语都得到练习。得分多的小组获胜。

活动扩展 教师任意说一个由j或q或x构成的音节，如“qián”，找到相应卡片的学生跑到一起，按顺序站成一排，然后把卡片举起来，一起重复教师说的音节。教师说音节的时候可以多重复几次，以便于学生能够听清楚。

MATERIALS NEEDED two sets of *pinyin* cards (including the tonal marks), some word cards containing *pinyin* j, q, and x.

METHOD Divide the students into two groups. Each group receives one set of the *pinyin* cards. The teacher puts the word cards on the board. The students start the game after the illustration on page 49 in the Student Book. The teacher points at a picture at random and the students are required to find the corresponding *pinyin* cards as soon as they can. Then they run to the front with the cards, arrange them according to the right sequence, hold the *pinyin* cards up, spell into the words like the ones on the cards and then read the syllables out loud together. The first group that has found the cards and has correctly spelled the words gets one point; the wrong group gets no point. The teacher is in charge of keeping the scores. Repeat the game till all the words on the cards get practiced. The group that gets more points wins in the end.

Exercise 练一练

A

- Listen and mark the tones. 听录音，标声调。

jia	quan	xiang	
qie	xue	qin	
xing	jiu	jun	qiong

Activity 课堂活动

B

- With three to six students in a group, find the *pinyin* cards and place them under the flash cards to make a word. 三到六个小朋友一组，把找到的拼音卡贴在相应的图片下边，拼成一个词语。

EXPANDED ACTIVITY The teacher says a syllable composed of j, q or x at random, for example, qián. The students who find the corresponding cards run toward one place, and stand in line according to the sequence. After that, they raise the cards, repeat the syllable said by the teacher. The teacher can repeat the syllable a few more times so that the students can hear him clearly.

A Let's recognize 认一认

这部分是本课学习的词语，教学方法参见本书的"使用说明"。

This section teaches the words in the lesson. Refer to the *Teacher Manual* for the teaching method in the book.

SUPPLEMENTARY WORDS[补充生词]

桃 táo peach | 梨 lí pear | 西瓜 xīguā water melon | 芒果 mángguǒ mango | 柠檬 níngméng lemon |

可乐 kělè Coke | 雪碧 xuěbì Sprite | 牛奶 niúnǎi milk | 酸奶 suānnǎi yogurt | 果汁 guǒzhī fruit juice

B Exercises 练一练

1. Listen, number the words, and mark the tones. 听录音，填序号，标声调。

KEY · · 答案

pínguǒ	xiāngjiāo	bōluó	pútáo	cǎoméi
5	3	1	2	4

录音文本：
1. bōluó 2. pútáo
3. xiāngjiāo 4. cǎoméi
5. píngguǒ

2. One fruit represents one letter. Write down the letters represented by each fruit to spell the name of a fruit. Then draw the fruit. 每种水果代表一个拼音字母。请根据水果的排列写出拼音，并画出相应的水果。

KEY · · 答案

píngguǒ pútáo xiāngjiāo

7

Let's recognize 认一认

A

香蕉
xiāngjiāo
banana

苹果
píngguǒ
apple

菠萝
bōluó
pineapple

吃
chī
eat

葡萄
pútáo
grape

草莓
cǎoméi
strawberry

喝
hē
drink

水
shuǐ
water

茶
chá
tea

50

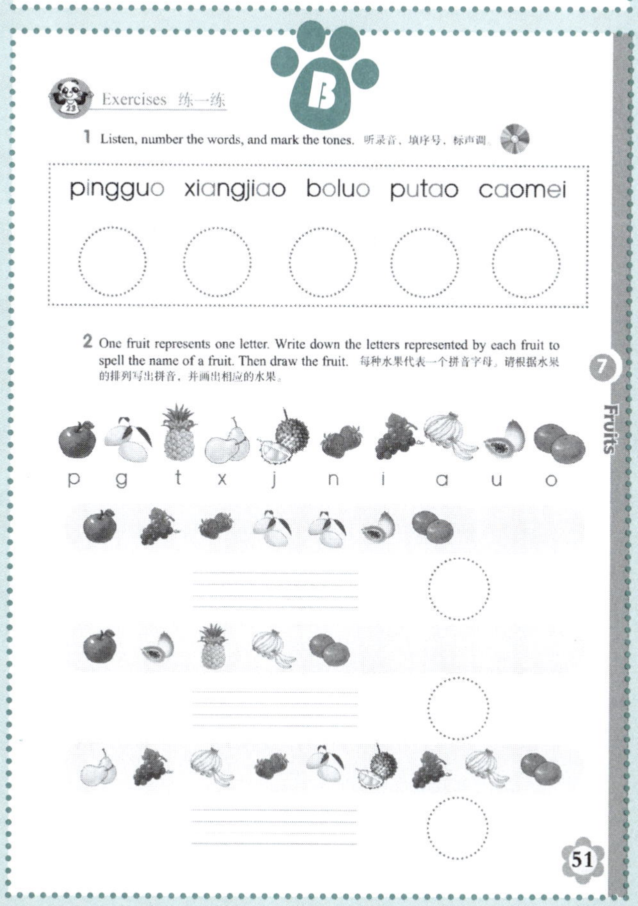
B

Exercises 练一练

1 Listen, number the words, and mark the tones. 听录音，填序号，标声调。

pingguo xiangjiao boluo putao caomei

2 One fruit represents one letter. Write down the letters represented by each fruit to spell the name of a fruit. Then draw the fruit. 每种水果代表一个拼音字母。请根据水果的排列写出拼音，并画出相应的水果。

p g t x j n i a u o

7 Fruits

51

Notes

A Activity 课堂活动

Write the 16 *pinyin* of words in the form in a random order. Listen to the recording and place a mark on the word you hear. The student who is the first to have 4 *pinyin* on one line wins the game. 先把下边16个词的拼音随意地抄写在表格中，然后听录音，在听到的词语上面画×，四个×形成一条直线就赢啦!

方法 按照学生用书第52页的图示做游戏。先让学生把16个词的拼音随意写在表格中，然后播放录音，让学生在听到的词语上画×。教师提示学生：如果表格中出现四个×连成的一条直线或者斜线，请举手示意。表格中最先形成一条直线或者斜线的学生获胜。

活动扩展 16个拼音可以换成以前学过的16个汉字，按上述规则做游戏。

METHOD Start the game after the illustration on page 52 in the Student Book. First, have the students fill in the *pinyin* for the 16 words in the chart randomly, and then play the recording. Have the students mark × on the words heard. The teacher reminds the students: if four × appearing in the chart and they form a linear line or a slant line, please raise your hand. The student wins if he first has the linear or the slant line showing in his chart.

EXPANDED ACTIVITY The 16 *pinyin* words can be changed into 16 characters learned before. Play the game after the above-mentioned rules.

B Let's say 说一说

教学方法参见本书的“使用说明”。

Refer to the *Teacher Manual* for the teaching method in the book.

7

Activity 课堂活动 A

- Write the 16 *pinyin* of words in the form in a random order. Listen to the recording and place a mark on the word you hear. The student who is the first to have 4 *pinyin* on one line wins the game. 先把下边16个词的拼音随意地抄写在表格中，然后听录音，在听到的词语上画×，四个×形成一条直线就赢啦！

píngguǒ shuǐ yǎnjing māma tóufa

bōluó kùzi lánsè xiāngjiāo hóngsè chá

jīntiān màozi pútáo xiāngjiāo nǎinai

Let's say 说一说 B

7 Fruits

Notes

Supplementary activities 补充活动

1. Help out 帮帮忙

准备材料 活动页（见附页7.1）

方法 复印足够数量的活动页，发给每个学生一份。在商店里，三只小动物找不到自己想要买的东西了。教师读三遍物品的名称，学生一边听一边将图下方的拼音补充完整，然后根据小动物手里的声母，帮它们找到要买的东西。先找到的同学请举手，告诉老师小猴、小猫和小象都想买什么东西。

物品名称 裙子、鸡蛋、鞋、橘子、西瓜、香蕉

MATERIALS NEEDED Activity Page (See attachment 7.1)

METHOD Make enough copies of the Activity Page. Give each student a copy. In the store, three little pets couldn't find what they want to buy. The teacher reads out the names of the things for three times. The students complete the *pinyin* in the picture while listening to the teacher, and then help the little animals find what they want to buy according to the initial letters in their hands. The student who finds them first raises his hand, and tells the teacher what monkey, cat and elephant want to buy.

NAMES OF THE COMMODITY See the Chinese version on the left.

2. The fruit picture 水果图

准备材料 词语卡片、白纸、彩笔、铅笔

方法 教师在黑板上贴上本课所学的水果的词语卡片，也可以准备水果实物，或者把这些水果画出来。每个学生用铅笔和彩笔在白纸上画出其中一种水果。教师将学生分成人数相等的两个大组，每组依次派一个学生去对方小组里取一张水果图。学生拿到图后，尽快在图上写出水果的名字（拼音或汉字均可），然后快速跑到教师面前把水果名称读出来。写得正确加1分，读得正

MATERIALS NEEDED word cards, white paper, color pens, pencils

METHOD The teacher pastes the word cards of fruits learned in this on the board. He can also prepare the fresh fruit, or draw the fruit on the board. Each student learns to draw a fruit on a piece of the white paper with the pencils and the color pens. Then the teacher puts the students into two big groups of equal number. Each group sends a student to get a fruit picture from the other group in turn. After that, they write the name of the fruit on the pic-

确再加1分，错误不加分。教师负责计时、计分。重复这个步骤，直到把对方的图拿完为止。在最短时间内得分最多的小组获胜。

ture (It can be in either *pinyin* or the characters). Then run to the teacher and read out the name of the fruit to him. If the student writes it correctly, he gets one point; if he reads it correctly, he gets another point; if he makes a mistake, he gets no point. The teacher is in charge of keeping the score, and the time. Repeat this step till all the pictures from the other group are taken. The group that gets the higher point in the shorter time wins in the end.

3. Make fruit head decorations 制作水果头饰

准备材料▶▶剪刀、白纸、铅笔、彩带、活动页（见附页7.3）

方法▶▶复印足够数量的活动页，每5~6名学生发一份。每个学生从本课所学的水果词中选择一个，按照图示做一个漂亮的水果头饰。做好后要保存起来，供下节课的表演唱使用。

MATERIALS NEEDED▶▶scissors, white paper, pencils, color ribbons, and Activity Page (See attachment 7.3)

METHOD▶▶Make enough copies of the Activity Page. Give 5 to 6 students a copy. Each student chooses a word of fruit from this lesson and makes a beautiful head decoration after the illustration. Keep it for use in singing for the next class.

8 I eat apples 我吃苹果

A Let's learn 学一学

❶ 这部分学习由“吃/喝”构成的动词谓语句，基本格式是：“主语＋吃/喝＋宾语”，例如“我吃草莓”，“老师喝水”。教学中要注意“吃”、“喝”与宾语的搭配。

❷ 教师提前准备一个苹果、一瓶水，以及本课的词语卡片。教师先拿出苹果，让学生说出苹果的中文名称，然后领读几遍。随后教师张大嘴，做出吃苹果的样子，动作可以夸张一些，同时对学生们说：“吃苹果”，让学生跟读。“吃苹果”的动作可以多做几次，每做一次动作就领读一次，直到学生熟练地掌握了这个短语。用同样的方法讲解“喝水”。

❸ 教师拿出本课的词语卡片，先把“吃”和“喝”的卡片分别贴到黑板的左边和右边，然后组织两个课堂活动：（1）教师举起一张卡片，如“香蕉”，让学生在黑板上指出正确的动词，同时做出“吃”的动作。以此类推，直到所有的词语都得到练习。（2）教师把水果和饮料的实物或卡片分发到学生的手中，每个学生根据自己手中的实物或者卡片，做出相应的“吃”或者“喝”的动作，然后大声说：“我吃/喝……”，教师给予积极的鼓励，同时重复学生的句子：“××

❶ This section teaches the predicate sentence composed of the verbs “吃” and “喝”. Its basic structure goes like this: “subject + 吃/喝 +object”. For example, “我吃草莓”, “老师喝水”. Pay attention to the combination of “吃” and “喝” with the objects.

❷ The teacher prepares an apple, a bottle of water and the word cards in the lesson beforehand. The teacher first takes out the apple, and then asks the students to say the Chinese name for the apple. Then lead the students in reading the name for a few times. After that, the teacher opens his mouth wide, making an exaggerated gesture of eating the apple. Say to the students: “吃苹果” and have them repeat after him. The apple-eating gesture can be done for many times. Lead in reading the term once every time the teacher makes the gesture till the students can speak the phrase fluently. Use the same way to explain “喝水”.

❸ The teacher takes out the word cards of the lesson. Put the cards of “吃” and “喝” on the left and right on the board respectively. The teacher can then organize two class activities: (1) the teacher raises a card, for example, “香蕉”. Have the students point at the right verb on

第8课 我吃苹果

wǒ chī píng guǒ

Let's learn 学一学

54

吃/喝……”。

❹教师让学生打开书，看图，听录音，跟读课本中的句子。这部分配有替换词语，可以用来进行替换练习。练习之前教师把句型“……吃/喝……”写在黑板上，随后教师指着替换部分的第一幅图做示范，先模仿儿童的声音说：“我吃草莓”，然后用正常的声音说：“弟弟/他吃草莓”，学生跟读。随后教师任意指一幅图，两个学生一组，分别以第一人称和第三人称说出句子。学生说完后，教师从头到尾读一遍替换的句子，学生跟读。

the board, and make a gesture of eating. Continue this way till all the words get practiced; (2) the teacher gives the fruits, drinks or the cards to the students. Every student makes a corresponding gesture either expressing eat or drink according to the real object or the cards in their hands, and then says loudly: “我吃/喝……” The teacher responds positively to the students' response and repeats the student's sentence at the same time: “××吃/喝……”

❹ The teacher asks the students to open their books, look at the picture, listen to the recording and read after the sentences in the lesson. This section is provided with substitute words which can be used for substitution drill. Before the drill, the teacher writes out the sentence pattern “……吃/喝……” on the board, and then points at the first picture in the substitution section for demonstration, imitating the children's voice and says: “我吃草莓”. After that he uses the normal voice and says: “弟弟/他吃草莓”. Have the students read after him. Then the teacher points at a picture at random, two students in a group, using both the first and third person pronouns to speak out the sentences respectively. After that, the teacher reads out the substitute sentences from the beginning to the end. The students follow him in the reading.

TEXT TRANSLATION[课文译文]

我吃苹果。I eat apples.

我喝水。I drink water.

B PATTERN'S SUBSTITUTE[句型替换]

我/弟弟吃草莓。 我/爸爸吃菠萝。 我/猴子吃香蕉。

我/妈妈吃葡萄。 我/爷爷喝茶。

Let's try 试一试

B

______ 吃/喝 ______ 。
chī / hē

Sing and perform 表演唱

歌曲的学习方法参见本书的“使用说明”。

活动方法 学生们学会歌曲以后，教师组织课堂活动：学生们拿出上一节课做的水果头饰，戴在头上，围成一圈。教师戴上一个苹果头饰，先做示范：“苹果，我是一个苹果，啦啦啦……”一边唱一边跳，动作可以自由发挥，气氛要活泼快乐。学生们根据自己头上戴的水果头饰，一个接一个地唱下去。

活动扩展 教师任选一个学生A，其他学生根据该学生戴的头饰围着他/她一边跳一边唱歌：“苹果，A是一个苹果，啦啦啦……”

歌曲文本 苹果，我是一个苹果。啦啦啦……菠萝，我是一个菠萝。啦啦啦……葡萄，我是一个葡萄。啦啦啦……香蕉，我是一个香蕉。啦啦啦……草莓，我是一个草莓。啦啦啦……

Refer to the *Teacher Manual* for the method for learning the song in the book.

ACTIVITY METHOD After the students have learned the song the teacher organizes the following class activity: the students take out the fruit head decorations prepared in the last class and put them around their heads, then stand in a circle. The teacher wears a fruit head decoration to do the demonstration: “苹果，我是一个苹果，啦啦啦……” He sings and dances at the same time. He can dance freely, the atmosphere should be lively. The students then start to sing one after the other according to the fruit on their head decorations.

EXPANDED ACTIVITY The teacher can pick up a student, for example, A. The other students then sings and dances around him/her according to his/her fruit head decoration: “苹果，A是一个苹果，啦啦啦……”

THE SONG SCRIPT Apple , I am an apple. La la la... Pineapple , I am a pineapple. La la la... Grape , I am a grape. La la la... Banana , I am a banana. La la la... Strawberry , I am a strawberry. La la la...

Sentence patterns 学句型

Read the patterns aloud, and then choose four of the pictures and compose four sentences with “吃” and “喝”. 大声朗读句型，然后选择四幅小图，用“吃”和“喝”造句。

❶ 这部分是句型总结与复习。教师先领学生反复大声朗读句型框里的句型，

❶ This section is the summary of the sentence patterns and the re-

8

Sing and perform 表演唱

A

Píngguǒ, wǒ shì yí ge píngguǒ.
Lā lā lā ......

Bōluó, wǒ shì yí ge bōluó.
Lā lā lā ......

Pútáo, wǒ shì yí ge pútáo.
Lā lā lā ......

Xiāngjiāo, wǒ shì yí ge xiāngjiāo.
Lā lā lā ......

Cǎoméi, wǒ shì yí ge cǎoméi.
Lā lā lā ......

56

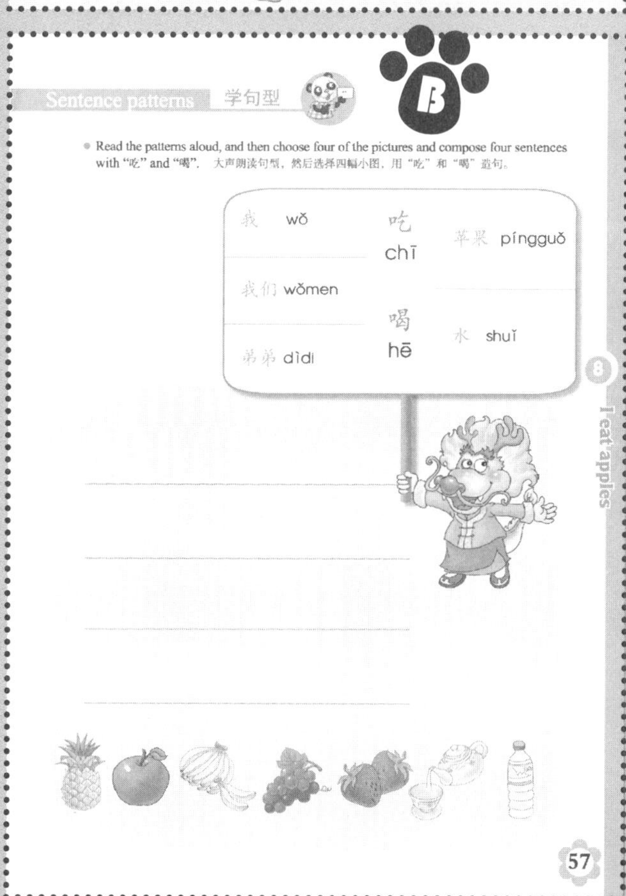

Sentence patterns 学句型

B

- Read the patterns aloud, and then choose four of the pictures and compose four sentences with "吃" and "喝". 大声朗读句型，然后选择四幅小图，用"吃"和"喝"造句。

我 wǒ	吃 chī	苹果 píngguǒ
我们 wǒmen		
弟弟 dìdi	喝 hē	水 shuǐ

8 I eat apples

57

Notes

直到学生可以流利地读出句型框里的四个句子。

❷ 学生看大框下边的水果和饮料图，用“……吃/喝……”造句，可以用拼音或者汉字写出自己喜欢吃的水果和喜欢喝的饮料，教师个别指导。学生做完练习后，教师找学生到教室前边，一边指小图，一边把自己写的句子读出来。

views. The teacher first leads the students in reading loud the sentence patterns in the box repeatedly. Read till the students can say the four sentences fluently in the sentence pattern box.

❷ The students look at the pictures of the fruit and drinks under the big frame, using “……吃/喝……” to make up sentences. They can use either *pinyin* or the characters to write out their favorite fruits and drinks. The teacher supervises individually. After the students have finished the exercise the teacher calls them to come to the front to read out the sentences they have written while pointing at the small picture.

A Interesting characters 趣味汉字

本课学习的汉字是“门”和“月”，要求学生掌握这两个字的正确写法。汉字的教学方法参见本书的“使用说明”。

This lesson teaches the characters “门” and “月”. The student are required to master the correct way of writing these two characters. Refer to the *Teacher Manual* for the teaching method in the book.

B Let's do it 做一做

Make a poster: A beautiful orchard 做招贴画：美丽的果园

准备材料 ➡ 苹果树、香蕉树、椰子树等当地果树的实景图片

方法 ➡ 如果所在学校开设有植物课，可以借助植物课的课本，让学生选择一种果树，画出一年中果树成长的不同阶段。教师也可以帮助学生从网上找一些果树成长的图片，做一张果园的海报。海报做好后，学生向全班同学展示自己的作品，同时让同学们猜猜树上结的是哪种水果。

常识介绍 ➡ 果树是指果实可以吃的树木。中国地域辽阔，温带、亚热带、热

MATERIALS NEEDED ➡ the actual pictures of the apple trees, the banana trees, and the coconut trees, etc.

METHOD ➡ If the school offers the Botany class, the students can select a tree from the textbooks. Then have them draw out the different stages of its growth during the year. The teacher can also help the students find some pictures showing the growth of the fruit trees on the Internet. Make a poster of an orchid. After that, the student displays his works to the whole class. Have them guess what fruit is on the tree.

8

A

Interesting characters 趣味汉字

door

门

mén

门 门 门 门

moon

月

yuè

月 月 月 月

58

B

Let's do it 做一做

• Make a poster: A beautiful orchard 做招贴画：美丽的果园

8 I eat apples

59

Notes

带的果树都有。从类型上讲，果树主要分为木本果树和草本果树两大类。木本果树由于所处地带不同，又分为常绿果树和落叶果树。南方热带和亚热带的果树，多为常绿果树；北方温带的果树，多为落叶果树。中国北方的果树大多是木本落叶果树，种类包括：（1）仁果类：苹果、梨、山楂等；（2）核果类：桃、李、杏、樱桃等；（3）浆果类：葡萄、猕猴桃等；（4）坚果类：核桃、榛子、栗子等；（5）其他果树类：柿子、枣、无花果、石榴等。中国南方主要的果树有：柑橘、香蕉、荔枝、龙眼、椰子、芒果、菠萝、橙、橄榄、木瓜、柠檬、柚子等。

COMMON SENSE INTRODUCTION Fruit trees refer to the tress whose fruits are edible. Being vast in its territory, China boasts off the fruit trees of various kinds in the different climates such as mild, sub tropical and tropical. From the view of the fruit trees, they are classified primarily into two major types: wooden and grassy. The wooden fruit trees are classified into the perennial and annual kinds depending on the regions they grow. In the tropical and sub tropical south, the trees are usually the type of evergreen nature; in the mild north, they are usually leaf falling. In the north, the fruit trees are primarily wood leaf falling types which are: (1) flesh bearing: apple, pear, and crataegus, etc. (2) core bearing: peach, plum, apricot, and berry, etc. (3) liquid bearing: grapes, kiwi, etc. (4) nuts: walnut, hazelnut, chestnut, etc. (5) other types: persimmon, dates, figs, pomegranate, etc. The major fruit trees in southern China include: tangerine, banana, lichen, longyan, mango, pineapple, orange, olive, papaya, lemon, grapefruit, etc.

Supplementary activities 补充活动

1. Paint, write and speak 涂一涂，写一写，说一说

准备材料 活动页（见附页8.1）

方法 复印活动页，发给每个学生一份。两个学生一组，先为自己喜欢的水果和饮料涂上颜色，然后用拼音或者汉字写出水果和饮料的名称，同时写上自己的名字。做好后，两人对比一下各自喜欢的水果和饮料有哪些相同、哪些不同，用"我吃/喝……"对话，教师个别指导。

MATERIALS NEEDED Activity Page (See attachment 8.1)

METHOD Make copies of the Activity Page. Give a copy to each student. Two students are in a group. Have them paint the colors on their favorite fruits and drinks, and then write down the names in either *pinyin* or the Chinese characters. After that, write down their names, and then compare to see the similarities and the differences between their favorite fruits and drinks. Use "我吃/喝……" to make a dialogue. The teacher supervises individually.

2. The fruit basket for the teacher 送给老师的水果篮

准备材料▶▶剪刀、胶水、活动页（见附页8.2）

方法▶▶复印足够数量的活动页，发给每个学生一份。让学生把附页8.1上涂了颜色的水果剪下来，粘贴到本页的水果篮中，在水果篮上写上自己的名字。然后学生将水果篮剪下来，送给老师，同时告诉老师水果篮里有哪些水果。下课后，教师可以用学生的作品做一期墙报。

MATERIALS NEEDED▶▶scissors, glue stick, Activity Page (See attachment 8.2)

METHOD▶▶Make enough copies of the Activity Page. Give a copy to each student. Have the students cut out the colored fruits from the Attachment 8.1, and then paste them onto the fruit basket on the page and write their names in the fruit basket. After that, have the students cut out the fruit basket and send it to the teacher. The students should tell the teacher what fruits there are in the basket. After the class, the teacher can use the students' works to make a fruit bulletin on the wall.

3. Ask and look for 问一问，找一找

准备材料▶▶活动页（见附页8.3）

方法▶▶复印足够数量的活动页。学生两人一组，一人拿A图，一人拿B图，互相不能看对方的图片。教师提示学生：在两张图中只有一个人（或动物）喜欢一样的水果（或者饮料），其他的都不一样。让学生通过对话找出喜欢相同水果（或者饮料）的人（或动物）。

对话示例▶▶A：杰克喜欢菠萝。

B：杰克喜欢苹果。

MATERIALS NEEDED▶▶Activity Page (See attachment 8.3)

METHOD▶▶Make enough copies of the Activity Page. Two students are in a group. One holds Picture A and one holds Picture B. They can't look at other's picture. The teacher prompts the students: there is only one person (or an animal) who likes the same fruits (or drinks) in the two pictures. All the others like different things. Have the students find the people (or animal) who like the same fruit (or drink) through the dialogue.

REVIEW 4 复习

A Look, find and draw 看一看，找一找，画一画

Place a √ mark on the fruits that Jack wants to buy. 在杰克想买的水果旁边画√。

方法 学生看图，根据杰克手中清单上写的四种水果名称帮助他找到想买的水果，在水果旁边的圆圈内画钩。随后两个学生一组，先互相检查对方的答案正确与否，然后通过对话了解在清单上的四种水果中，同伴喜欢吃哪种，最后把自己喜欢的和同伴喜欢的水果画出来。做得又快又好的学生可以得到一个小奖励。

对话示例 A：你喜欢吃什么？

B：我喜欢吃苹果。

METHOD Looking at the picture, the students write out the names of the four fruits on Jack's shopping list and help him find the fruits he wants to buy. Tick in the circles by the fruits. Then put two students in a group. Have them check each other if their answers are correct. Then get to know which fruit on Jack's shopping list is the partner's favorite through the dialogue. Finally, have the students write out the fruits that both he and his partner like. The student who finishes both fast and best can get a small prize.

EXAMPLE See the Chinese version on the left.

B Story time 故事会

教学方法参见本书的“使用说明”。

故事文本 兰兰不在家。小猫跑到厨房，打开冰箱，看见冰箱里有很多水果。小猫真高兴，它说：“哇！真多啊！”小猫拿起一根香蕉吃了起来，一边吃一边说：“香蕉真好吃！”兰兰回家了，找不到小猫，她很奇怪，说：“猫在哪里？”最后，兰兰来到厨房，看到冰箱门开着，小猫正坐在冰箱里吃苹果呢。它已经冻得发抖了，可还在说：“苹果真好吃！”唉！

Refer to the *Teacher Manual* for the teaching method in the book.

STORY TEXT Lanlan was not at home. The little cat ran into the kitchen. He opened the refrigerator, and saw so many fruits inside. He was really happy and said, “哇！真多啊！” He took a banana and started to eat. He said: “香蕉真好吃？” while eating. When Lanlan came back home, she couldn't find the little cat. She felt very strange, and said: “猫在哪里？” Finally, Lanlan came to the kitchen, and saw the refrigerator's door was open. The little cat was eating the apple

Review 4 (复习4)

A

1 Look, find, and draw 看一看，找一找，画一画

- Place a √ mark on the fruits that Jack wants to buy. 在杰克想买的水果旁边画√。

- Which of the fruits that Jack bought do you and your partner like? Please draw them in the following photo frames. 在杰克买的水果中，你和你的同伴喜欢吃哪种？把它们画出来吧！

my favorite fruits | my partner's favorite fruits

60

2 Story time 故事会

B

61

Notes

there. He was already shivering with cold, but still kept saying: “苹果真好吃！” Hey!

TRANSLATION[译文] 图1：哇！真多啊！Wow! There are so many fruits!

图2：香蕉真好吃！The banana tastes so good!

图3：猫在哪里？Where is the cat?

图4：苹果真好吃！The apple tastes so good!

Unit Five 第五单元

第九课： 场所
第十课： 奶奶在花园

教学目标：
Objectives
❶ 拼音：z c s
❷ 句型：……在……

生词：
New Words
饭厅・书房・厨房・卫生间・花园・客厅・卧室・在

语言点：
Language Point
由“在”构成的动词谓语句

日常用语：
Daily Expressions
A：我住在北京。你住在哪里？
B：我住在纽约。

汉字：
Chinese Characters
叉 女

活动：
Activity
设计漂亮的房子

Introduction 导入

❶ 如果有条件，教师准备一些当地人常吃的食物，如鸡蛋、麦片、三明治、汉堡包、香蕉、牛奶、酸奶、水，等等。教师先把食物藏到桌子下边。上课时，教师一边说“今天我吃……”，一边拿出食物。例如，教师说“今天我吃鸡蛋”，随后从桌子下边拿出鸡蛋展示给学生，以此类推，直到把所有的食物都摆到桌子上面。教师展示完以后，让学生逐个到教室前边，一边拿起自己想吃的食物，一边说句子。以此复习前一个单元学习的内容。如果没有条件，教师可以用词语卡片或者自己画图代替实物。

❷ 教师准备本课的词语卡片，粘贴在黑板上。教师先做动作，如睡觉、吃饭、刷牙、看书、拿着遥控器看电视等，学生猜出这些动作发生的场所，然后到黑板前指出相应的卡片，并试着读出卡片上的拼音。学生练完以后，教师一边做动作，一边指卡片，领读词语，学生跟读。学生熟悉了本课的场所名称后，教师可以组织两个小游戏：（1）教师做动作，学生用中文说出场所名称；（2）教师指卡片，说场所名称，学生做动作。

❶ If possible, the teacher prepares some local foods such as eggs, oats meal, sandwiches, McDonald, banana, sour milk, water, etc before the class. The teacher first hides the foods under the desk. When class starts, the teacher takes the foods out while saying “今天我吃……” For example, “今天我吃鸡蛋”, and then takes out the egg from under the desk to show it to the students. Follow this way till all the foods are displayed on the desk. After that, have the students come to the front, saying the names of the foods while picking up the foods they like to eat. This activity is used to review the previous unit. If it’s impossible, the teacher can use the word cards or the pictures drawn by himself to replace the real objects.

❷ The teacher prepares the word cards for the lesson and sticks them onto the board. The teacher makes the gestures first, such as sleep, eat, brush teeth, read a book, and take a remote control to watch TV. Have the students guess the places where these actions take place and then have them come to the board to point at the corresponding cards, and try to read out the *pinyin* on the cards. After that, the teacher points at the cards while making the gestures. The teacher leads in reading the words and the students follow him. After the students get familiar with the names of the places taught in the lesson, the teacher can organize two little games: (1) the teacher makes gestures and the students say their names in Chinese; (2) the teacher points at the cards and says the places’ names, the students make the gestures.

第 9 课 场所
chǎng suǒ

Let's read 读一读

Z z zāng

C c cǎo

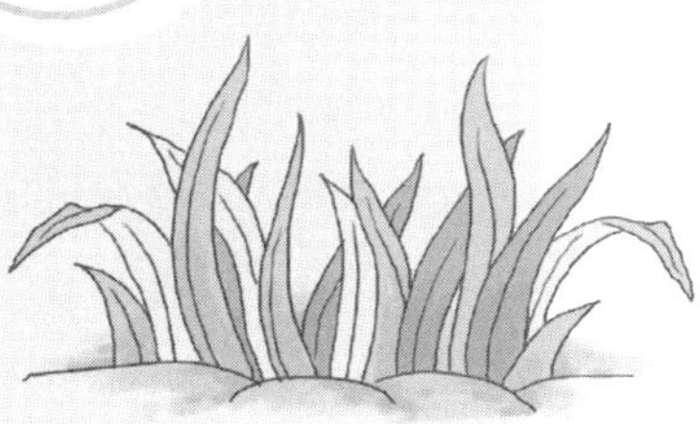

S s sǎn

62

Notes

Places 场所 9

A Let's read 读一读

❶ 学习声母 z、c、s 的读音。

❷ 学习 z、c、s 与韵母的拼合。

❶ Learn the pronunciations of the initials z, c, and s.

❷ Learn the combination of the initials z, c, s and the finals.

Exercise 练一练

Listen and place a √ mark on the *pinyin* you hear. 听录音，在听到的拼音前面画√。

KEY · · 答案

sān cè zì zuǐ cāng sōng

Activity 课堂活动

With two students in a group, one reads the initial and one reads the final. Try to find out how many syllables the *pinyin* letters can make. Write the number in the circle.
两个小朋友一组，一人读声母，一人读韵母。看一看下边的拼音可以组成多少个音节，把数字写到圆圈里。

方法 教师将声母 z、c、s 和韵母 a、e、i、u 打乱顺序写在黑板上，然后按照学生用书第63页的图示做游戏。两个学生一组，一人读声母，一人读韵母，一起数数这七个拼音字母一共可以组成多少个音节，把数字写到圆圈里。学生完成后，教师在黑板上任指一个声母和一个韵母，找学生快速拼读出音节。

活动扩展 教师可以增加声母和韵母的数量，加大练习的难度。

METHOD The teacher writes out the initials z, c, s, and the finals a, e, i, u out of order on the board. Start the game after the illustration on page 63. Two students are in a group, one reads the initials and the other reads the finals. Then count with the partner how many syllables these seven *pinyin* letters can make in total, and then fill in the number in the circle. After that, the teacher points at an initial and a final at random and asks the students to read out the syllable quickly.

EXPANDED ACTIVITY Increase the number of the initials and the finals to make the exercise more difficult.

Exercise 练一练 A

- Listen and place a √ mark on the *pinyin* you hear. 听录音，在听到的拼音前画√。

- zān
- sān

- sè
- cè

- cì
- zì

- zuǐ
- cuǐ

- cāng
- sāng

- cōng
- sōng

9 Places

Activity 课堂活动 B

- With two students in a group, one reads the initial and one reads the final. Try to find out how many syllables the *pinyin* letters can make. Write the number in the circle. 两个小朋友一组，一人读声母，一人读韵母。看一看下边的拼音可以组成多少个音节，把数字写到圆圈里。

A Let's recognize 认一认

这部分是本课学习的词语，教学方法参见本书的“使用说明”。

This section teaches the words in the lesson. Refer to the *Teacher Manual* for the teaching method in the book.

B Exercises 练一练

1. Listen and match. 听录音，连线。

KEY · 答案

录音文本：

1. 爷爷在客厅。 2. 奶奶在花园。 3. 妹妹在饭厅。
4. 弟弟在卧室。 5. 爸爸在书房。 6. 妈妈在厨房。

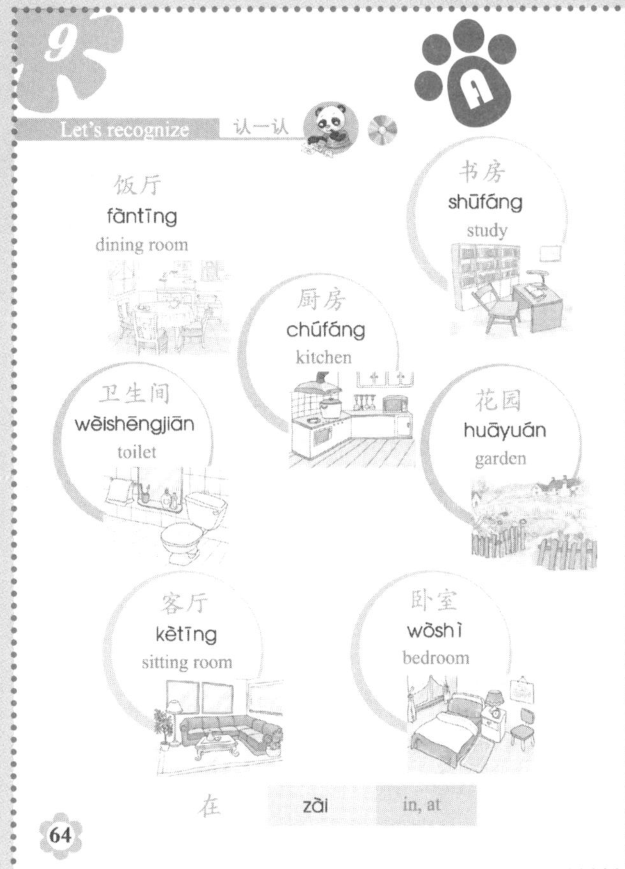

9

A

Let's recognize 认一认

饭厅
fàntīng
dining room

书房
shūfáng
study

厨房
chúfáng
kitchen

卫生间
wèishēngjiān
toilet

花园
huāyuán
garden

客厅
kètīng
sitting room

卧室
wòshì
bedroom

在 zài in, at

64

B

Exercises 练一练

1 Listen and match. 听录音，连线。

wòshì huāyuán kètīng fàntīng chúfáng shūfáng

2 Copy the *pinyin* names of the rooms. Then draw one thing in each photo frame that belongs in the room. 抄写拼音，看看这是什么房间，然后画出这个房间里的一个物品。

wèishēngjiān ____ kètīng ____

chúfáng ____ wòshì ____

9 Places

65

Notes

A Activity 课堂活动

Ask your partner in which room are the following things put in his/her family? Write the numbers in the blank under the picture of the room. 问问你的同伴，下面这些物品放在他/她家的哪个房间里？把物品的序号填在相应的房间图下边吧！

方法 按照学生用书第66页的图示做游戏。两个学生一组，学生A任指一个物品图，如“书”，学生B用中文说出该物品放在自己家里的哪个房间，如“（书）在书房”。学生A将“书”的序号“1”写在图画“书房”下边的空格里。学生A填写完所有的物品序号后，学生B指图，学生A回答。学生完成后，教师任指物品图，让学生A（或B）说出该物品在学生B或A家里的哪个房间。本题中的物品名称大多数还没有学，教师可根据实际情况进行教学。如果学生水平较低，物品名称可以忽略，学生指图即可；如果学生水平较高，教师可以将其作为补充词语教给学生。

补充词语 书、漱口杯、牙刷、电脑、餐具、沙发、锅、床、卫生纸、喷水壶、台灯、花瓶、花、草

METHOD Start the game according to the illustration on page 66 in the Student Book. Two students are in a group. Student A points at an object picture, for example, *book*. Student B then uses Chinese to say the place where the object is in his house, for example, “（书）在书房”. Student A then puts the serial number 1 of the *book* in the blank under the “书房”. After Student A has finished filling all the serial numbers for the objects Student B points at the picture and writes down the serial numbers for Student A to answer this time. After that, the teacher points at an object picture at random and asks Student A (or B) to say where the object in Student B's or A's house is. Most of the object names in the lesson have not been learned so the teacher can teach them according to the actual situation. If the students are not advanced with Chinese, the object names can be omitted; otherwise, the teacher can use them as the supplementary words in his teaching.

SUPPLEMENTARY WORDS book, mouth rinsing glass, tooth brush, computer, dining silverware, sofa, wok, bed, toilet paper, water spraying kettle, floor lamp, vase, flower and grass

B Let's say 说一说

教学方法参见本书的“使用说明”。

替换词语 这部分提供了四个城市名称，可以用来替换对话中的“北京”和“纽约”。

Refer to the *Teacher Manual* for the teaching method in the book.

SUBSTITUTE WORDS This section provides the names of four cities which can be used to replace “北京” and “纽约” in the dialogue.

9
Activity 课堂活动
A
Ask your partner in which room are the following things put in his /her family? Write the numbers in the blank under the picture of the room. 问问你的同伴，下面这些物品放在他/她家的哪个房间里？把物品的序号填在相应的房间图下边吧！
1 2 3 4 5 6
7 8 9 10 11 12
厨房 chúfáng
书房 shūfáng
卧室 wòshì
卫生间 wèishēngjiān
客厅 kètīng
花园 huāyuán
66

Let's say 说一说
B
1 我住在北京。你住在哪里？
Wǒ zhù zài Běijīng. Nǐ zhù zài nǎlǐ?
I live in Beijing. Where do you live?
2 我住在纽约。
Wǒ zhù zài Niǔyuē.
I live in New York.
9 Places
巴黎
Bālí
Paris
马德里
Mǎdélǐ
Madrid
东京
Dōngjīng
Tokyo
首尔
Shǒu'ěr
Seoul
67

Notes

Supplementary activities 补充活动

1. Look and read 找一找，读一读

准备材料 活动页（见附页9.1）

方法 复印足够数量的活动页，发给每个学生一份。学生在最短的时间内找出活动页上的儿歌里有几个z，几个c，几个s，并把数字写到儿歌下边的空心圆里。写完的学生举手，给老师读一遍儿歌。教师检查结果，全部数对的学生可以得到一个小奖励。最后，教师领读儿歌，凡是有z，c，s的地方要重读，以加深学生的印象。

MATERIALS NEEDED Activity Page (See attachment 9.1)

METHOD Make copies of the Activity Page. Give each student a copy. Have the students find how many z, c, and s in the children song on the Activity Page in the shortest time possible. Write down these numbers in the blank circles under the children song. After done, the student raises his hand, and reads the song to the teacher. The teacher checks their findings. The student who makes no mistakes can get a small prize. At the end, the teacher leads the students in reading the children song. Stress the places where z, c, and s appear in order to make deeper impression on the students.

2. Grab the cards 抢卡片

准备材料 活动页（见附页9.2）

方法 教师将活动页中的词语剪下来，随意摆放在一张桌子上边，学生围在桌旁。教师说卡片上的一个词语，学生要迅速找到该词语并将卡片拿起来。拿对卡片的学生把卡片留在自己手里，拿错卡片的学生要回到座位上，退出这个游戏。抢到最多卡片的学生获胜，可以得到一个小奖励。

MATERIALS NEEDED Activity Page (See attachment 9.2)

METHOD The teacher cuts out the words from the Activity Page and spreads them on a desktop at random. Have the students stand around the desk. The teacher then starts to say a word on the card. The students should find the card with the word quickly and raise it up. The students who take the right cards can keep them while the students who take the wrong cards should return to their seats to exit from the game. The student who grabs the most cards wins in the end and can get a small prize.

3. Stick and paint 贴一贴，涂一涂

准备材料 ➧ 剪刀、胶棒、活动页（见附页9.3a和9.3b）

方法 ➧ 复印足够数量的活动页，发给每个学生一份。学生把9.3a上的物品图剪下来，然后按照自己的想法把物品图粘贴在9.3b上不同的房间里，最后为图画涂上漂亮的颜色。完成后，每人向大家介绍一下自己的作品。下课以后，教师可以跟学生们一起做一期漂亮的墙报。

MATERIALS NEEDED ➧ scissors, glue sticks, Activity Page (See attachment 9.3a and 9.3b)

METHOD ➧ Make enough copies of the Activity Page. Give each student a copy. Have the students cut out the pictures of the objects from the page 9.3a, and then stick them in the different rooms on page 9.3b according to their ideas. Finally, paint them with beautiful colors. After done, the student introduces his/her works to the class one by one. After the class, teacher can make a beautiful wall bulletin together with the students.

10 Grandma is in the garden 奶奶在花园

A Let's learn 学一学

❶ 这部分学习由“在”构成的动词谓语句，基本格式是“主语＋在＋场所名词”，表示某人或某物在某处，例如：“我在书房”，“猫在花园”。教师可以同时教给学生这个句型的否定形式，即“主语＋不在＋场所名词”，例如：“奶奶不在厨房”。

❷ 教师利用本课的词语卡片展示句型，如拿出“书房”的卡片，挡住自己的脸，同时说“老师在书房”或者“我在书房”，然后把卡片藏到身后，同时说“老师不在书房”或者“我不在书房”。“在”、“不在”和“书房”要重读，以引起学生注意。学生掌握了这种方法以后，教师换一张卡片，先挡住脸，再藏到身后，学生根据教师的动作说出句子，随后教师马上重复正确的句子，学生跟读，直到所有的词语都得到练习。如果时间允许，教师也可以让学生拿卡片，教师说句子，学生模仿教师做动作。

❸ 教师让学生打开书，看图，听录音，跟读课本中的句子。这部分配有替换词语，可以用来进行替换练习。练习之前教师把句型“……在……”写在黑板上，然后教师把课本举起来，指着替换部分的第一幅图做示范，说：“妈妈在厨房”，学生跟读。随后教师任意指

❶ This section teaches the predicate sentence composed of in, whose basic structure is “subject + 在 + place name”, expressing someone is in somewhere. For example, “我在书房”, “猫在花园”. The teacher can also teach the negative form of this sentence pattern at the same time, i.e., “subject + 不在 + place name”. For example, “奶奶不在厨房”.

❷ The teacher uses the word cards from the lesson to show the sentence pattern, for example, taking the card with the word “书房” on it, using it to block his face, and says: “老师在书房” or “我在书房”. Then he hides the card behind his back, and says at the same time: “老师不在书房” or “我不在书房”. Stress “在”, “不在”, and “书房” to draw the students' attention. After the students have learned the method, the teacher changes another card, first, blocks his face, and then hides it behind his back. The students say out the sentences according to the teacher's actions. The teacher repeats the correct sentence immediately. The students follow him till all the words get practiced. If time permits, the teacher can have the students take the cards, the teacher says the sentences, and asks the students to imitate the teacher's

第10课 奶奶在花园

nǎi nai zài huā yuán

A

Let's learn 学一学

一幅图，让学生说出句子。为了增加练习的难度，教师可以让学生合上课本，教师说人名，如“妈妈”，学生凭记忆抢答说“妈妈在厨房”。答得又快又好的学生得到鼓励或者奖励。

actions.

❸ The teacher asks the students to open their books, look at the pictures, listen to the recording, and read the sentences in the lesson following the recording. This section has the substitute words which can be used for the substitution drill. Before the exercise, the teacher writes down the sentence pattern “……在……” on the board, then raises the textbook, pointing at the first picture in the substitute section to do a demonstration: “妈妈在厨房。” The students follow him. Then the teacher points at a picture randomly, and asks the students to say the sentences. To increase the difficult level of the exercise, the teacher can ask the students to close their books. The teacher then starts to say the person's name, for example, “妈妈”; the students compete to answer by memory: “妈妈在厨房”. The students who answer faster and better can get encouragement or prizes.

TEXT TRANSLATION[课文译文]

奶奶在花园。Grandma is in the garden.

B

PATTERN'S SUBSTITUTE[句型替换]

妈妈在厨房。爸爸在书房。
狗在客厅。她/妹妹/姐姐在卫生间。
他/她/弟弟/妹妹在卧室。她/妹妹/姐姐在饭厅。

Let's try 试一试 B

______在______。
zài

chúfáng

shūfáng

kètīng

wèishēngjiān

wòshì

fàntīng

A Guess and sing 猜一猜，唱一唱

歌曲的学习方法参见本书的“使用说明”。

准备材料 准备几件日常生活用品，如书、勺子、盘子、花、牙刷、笔、毛巾等。

方法 学生们学会歌曲以后，教师组织课堂活动：将物品摆放在桌子上，两个学生一组，站在桌子旁边。教师将学生的眼睛蒙上，或者让学生闭上眼睛。教师说“开始”，两个学生从桌子上各拿起一件物品，根据物品猜出房间的名称，同时唱歌：“这是厨房。这是厨房。啦啦啦啦啦啦。××（学生自己的名字）在厨房，××在厨房，啦啦啦啦啦啦。”两个学生都唱完后，把眼睛睁开，并举起手中的物品，全班同学根据他们手中的物品，一起唱一遍歌曲。

歌曲文本 这是厨房。这是厨房。啦啦啦啦啦啦。丁丁在厨房。丁丁在厨房。啦啦啦啦啦啦。这是花园。这是花园。啦啦啦啦啦啦。美美在花园。美美在花园。啦啦啦啦啦啦。

Refer to the *Teacher Manual* for the method for learning the song in the book.

MATERIALS NEEDED prepare a few daily life objects, such as a book, a ladle, a plate, flower, a tooth brush, a pen, or a towel, etc.

METHOD After the students have learned the song, the teacher starts to organize the class activity: put the objects on the desk. Two students are in a group, stand around the desk. The teacher puts the blindfolds around the students' eyes or asks the students to close their eyes. The teacher then says “开始 (start)”. Two students each take a different object from the desk, guess the room's names according to the objects in their hands, and sing at the same time: “这是厨房。这是厨房。啦啦啦啦啦啦。×× (student's own name) 在厨房，××在厨房，啦啦啦啦啦啦。” After the two students finish singing, they open their eyes, raise the objects in their hands, the whole call starts to sing the song according to the objects in their hands.

THE SONG SCRIPT This is the kitchen. This is the kitchen. Lalalalalala. Dingding is in the kitchen. Dingding is in the kitchen. Lalalalalala. This is the garden. This is the garden. Lalalalalala. Meimei is in the garden. Meimei is in the garden. Lalalalalala.

10

Guess and sing 猜一猜，唱一唱

Zhè shì chúfáng.
Zhè shì chúfáng.
Lā lā lā lā lā lā.
Dīngdīng zài chúfáng.
Dīngdīng zài chúfáng.
Lā lā lā lā lā lā.

Zhè shì huāyuán.
Zhè shì huāyuán.
Lā lā lā lā lā lā.
Měiměi zài huāyuán.
Měiměi zài huāyuán.
Lā lā lā lā lā lā.

70

B Sentence patterns 学句型

Read the patterns aloud, and then look at the pictures and compose sentences with "在". 大声朗读句型，然后看图用"在"造句。

❶ 这部分是句型总结与复习。教师先领学生反复大声朗读句型框里的句型，直到学生可以流利地读出句型框里的句子。

❷ 学生看图，用句型"……在……"造句，可以用拼音或者汉字写出答案。学生做完练习后，教师检查，对全做对的学生给予鼓励或者奖励。随后教师任意指图，找学生大声读出答案；或者教师说句子，如"猫在客厅"，"猫在卧室"，学生根据课本上的图画判断对错，点头回答"对"，摇头回答"不对"。

❶ This section is the summary of the sentence patterns and the reviews. The teacher first leads the students in reading out loud the sentence patterns in the box till the students can read out the four sentences in the box fluently.

❷ The students look at the picture using the sentence pattern "……在……" to make up sentences. They can write out the answers in either *pinyin* or the characters. After the students finish up the exercise, the teacher checks their answers. Encourage or reward the students who are perfect with their answers. After that, the teacher points at a picture at random, and asks the student to read out loud the answers; or the teacher speaks sentences, for example, "猫在客厅", "猫在卧室". The students decide if the answers are correct based on the pictures on the book. They nod their heads to mean "对" (Yes), shake their heads to mean "不对" (Not right).

KEY · · 答案

它/鸟在卧室。 它们/猫在客厅。 它们/鸟在饭厅。 它/猫在卫生间。

Sentence patterns 学句型

B

- Read the patterns aloud, and then look at the pictures and compose sentences with "在". 大声朗读句型，然后看图用"在"造句。

他 tā	在 zài	客厅 kètīng
他们 tāmen		卧室 wòshì

....

....

....

....

Interesting characters 趣味汉字

本课学习的汉字是“叉”和“女”，要求学生掌握这两个字的正确写法。汉字的教学方法参见本书的“使用说明”。

This lesson teaches the characters “叉” and “女”. The students are required to master the correct way of writing these two characters. Refer to the *Teacher Manual* for the teaching method in the book.

Let's do it 做一做

Design a beautiful house with your partners. 跟你的同伴们一起设计一幢漂亮的房子吧。

准备材料 ➡ 铅笔、彩笔、彩纸、胶棒等

方法 ➡ 根据学生数量，将学生分为2~3人一组，一起设计一幢漂亮的房子。学生可以分工合作，如一人设计轮廓，一人涂色，一人装饰房子外边的环境。除了用铅笔、彩笔画图以外，学生也可以用彩纸剪出花、树、动物等，粘贴到图上。每个学生都要在同伴们的帮助下设计一幢房子。学生可以在课本上画图，也可以另外找一张白纸画图。学生的作品完成以后，教师可以组织一个全班的作品展览。

MATERIALS NEEDED ➡ pencils, color pens, color paper, glue sticks, etc.

METHOD ➡ Put the students into groups of two or three according to their numbers. They design a beautiful house together. They can divide their roles, for example, one is responsible for designing the outline of the house, one for painting, one for decorating the environment outside of the house. Besides pencils, color pens, they can also cut out the flowers, trees, animals, etc from the color papers, then paste them onto the picture. Every student is required to design a house with the help from his fellow students. They can draw on the books or on a separate piece of white paper. After all are done the teacher can organize an exhibition for the works of the whole class.

10

Interesting characters 趣味汉字

A

叉 叉

fork chā

叉 叉 叉 叉

女

girl nǚ

女 女 女 女

72

B

Let's do it 做一做

• Design a beautiful house with your partners. 跟你的同伴们一起设计一种漂亮的房子吧。

10 Grandma is in the garden

73

Notes

Supplementary activities 补充活动

1. Mysterious boxes 神秘的盒子

准备材料»一些空白卡片、两个空盒子，一个装着卡片“在”的盒子

方法»课前教师需要准备足够数量的卡片“在”，放在一个盒子里，然后在另外两个空盒子上分别写上“人物(people)”和“场所(place)”。上课时，教师先发给每个学生两张空白卡片，让学生在卡片上依次写出名字（自己或者他人的名字均可）和场所名词（用拼音或汉字均可），例如：“美美”、“客厅”。写完以后，学生按类别将两张卡片分别放在两个空盒子里。教师找学生从三个盒子里各摸出一张卡片，用卡片上的词连成一句话，并读出来。读得正确的学生可以留下卡片，读得不正确的学生要把卡片放回到盒子里。重复这个游戏，直到盒子里的卡片都被拿完。最后数一数，得到最多卡片的学生获胜。

MATERIALS NEEDED» some blank cards, two empty boxes, a box with the card “在”

METHOD» The teacher prepares enough cards with “在” on them before the class, puts them in a box, then writes *people* (人物) and *place* (场所) on the other two empty boxes. When in class, the teacher first hands out two blank cards to each student, then have them write out the people's names (their own names or other people's names) and the place names in turn, for example: “美美”, “客厅” (either by *pinyin* or by Chinese Characters). After that, the students put the two cards into the two empty boxes by category. The teacher asks a student to take one card from each of the three boxes, and uses the words in the cards to make up one sentence, and speaks it out. The students who read the sentence correctly can keep the card. Otherwise, put the cards back to the boxes. Repeat the game till all the cards in the boxes are taken. The student who gets the most cards wins in the end.

2. Look for the same picture 找相同

准备材料»活动页（见附页10.2）

方法»复印足够数量的活动页。两个学生一组，一人拿A图，一人拿B图，互相不能看对方的图片。教师提示学生在两张图中只有一幅小图完全一样，其他小图都有不一样的地方，让学生通过

MATERIALS NEEDED» Activity Page (See attachment 10.2)

METHOD» Make enough copies of the Activity Page. Two students are in a group. One holds Picture A and the other holds Picture B. They can't look at other's picture. The teacher

对话找出那幅完全相同的小图来。

对话示例➡A：美美在花园。

B：美美在客厅。

reminds the students that there is only one card that is identical between the two cards. All the others are different. Have the students discover the identical card through dialogue.

EXAMPLE➡See the Chinese version on the left.

3. Quick memory 快速记忆

准备材料➡表示家人和动物的词语卡片、活动页（见附页10.3）

方法➡复印活动页。把学生分成数量均等的若干组，发给每组一份活动页，让学生在30秒内记住活动页中九幅小图的内容，然后教师把活动页收上来，测试一下学生的记忆力。教师分别举起“爸爸”、“妈妈”、“爷爷”、“奶奶”、“姐姐”、“弟弟”、“妹妹”、“猫”、“狗”的词语卡片，并说出相应的中文名称，每组学生根据记忆抢答这些人或动物在哪个房间，如“奶奶在花园”。回答正确加1分，回答错误不加分。每组只有三次出错的机会，如果超过三次就不能参加抢答比赛了。做完游戏后，得分最多的小组获胜，教师给予鼓励或者奖励。

MATERIALS NEEDED➡the word cards showing the family members and the animals, Activity Page (See attachment 10.3)

METHOD➡Make copies of the Activity Page. Put the students into many groups of equal number. Give each group a copy of the Activity Page, and have them memorize the contents of the nine small pictures in 30 seconds, then the teacher collects the Activity Pages to test the students' memory. The teacher raises the cards with “爸爸”, “妈妈”, “爷爷”, “奶奶”, “姐姐”, “弟弟”, “妹妹”, “猫”, “狗”, reads out their names in Chinese. Each group competes to answer where these people or animals are by their memory. For example, “奶奶在花园”. The right answer gets one point; the wrong one gets no point. Each group, however, is given only three times for mistakes. Beyond three times, they are disqualified. At the end of the game, the group with the most points wins. The teacher gives encouragement or rewards.

REVIEW 5 复习

A Find and write 找一找，写一写

方法 ▶ 学生根据所给六个小朋友的服装和外貌特征，找到这些人都在哪个房间，并用拼音或汉字完成下边的句子。教师个别指导、检查，对全做对的学生给予鼓励。

METHOD ▶ The students find the rooms these six little friends in based on their clothes and physical features. Complete the following sentences either in *pinyin* or the characters. The teacher supervises individually and checks the answers. The perfect students should be given encouragement.

KEY · · 答案

丁丁在厨房。 美美在饭厅。 飞飞在书房。
杰克在卧室。 美美在卫生间。 婷婷在客厅。

B Story time 故事会

教学方法参见本书的“使用说明”。

故事文本 ▶ 老鼠哥哥和老鼠弟弟玩捉迷藏游戏。老鼠哥哥藏了起来，老鼠弟弟蒙着眼睛数数：“1，2，3……”数到10，它就开始找哥哥了。它先跑到客厅，没有找到。老鼠弟弟说：“它不在客厅。”它跑到卫生间，还是没有找到。老鼠弟弟说：“它不在卫生间。它在哪里？”原来，老鼠哥哥藏在厨房的垃圾桶里了。看见弟弟找不到自己，它得意地小声说：“嘻嘻，我在这里。”这时，女主人来了，“哗啦哗啦”，她往垃圾桶里倒了很多垃圾，老鼠哥哥被压在了下边。老鼠弟弟来到厨房，看见

Refer to the *Teacher Manual* for the teaching method in the book.

STORY TEXT ▶ The Big Brother Rat was playing the hide and seek with his little brother. The Big Brother Rat hid himself first. The Little Brother Rat started to count with his eyes shut: “1, 2, 3...” When he counted to ten, he started to look for his Big Brother. He ran into the living room first. Not there. The Little Brother Rat said: “它不在客厅。” He then ran to the bathroom. Not there either. The Little Brother Rat said: “它不在卫生间。它在哪里？” It turned out that the Big Brother Rat hid himself in the trashcan in the kitchen. Seeing his Little Brother

Review 5 (复习5)

A

1 Find and write 找一找，写一写

Dīngdīng zài ________.	Měimei zài ________.
________ zài shūfáng.	Jiékè zài ________.
________ zài wèishēngjiān.	Tíngting zài ________.

74

B

2 Story time 故事会

75

Notes

老鼠哥哥满头垃圾，郁闷地说：“我在这里。”老鼠弟弟偷着笑起来。

couldn't find him, he said: “嘻嘻，我在这里。” Just at this time, the mistress came in. She dumped a lot of garbage into the trash can. The Big Brother Rat was down there buried in the dirty trash. When the Little Brother Rat came into the kitchen, and saw his Big Brother full of trash. The Big Brother Rat said sadly: “我在这里。” The Little Brother Rat chuck-led to himself.

TRANSLATION[译文] 图1：1，2，3…… One, two, three...

图2：它不在客厅。It is not in the living room.

图3：它不在卫生间。它在哪里？It is not in the bathroom. Where is it?

图4：嘻嘻，我在这里。Xixi, I am here.

图6：我在这里。I am here.

TEACHER BOOK 2

Unit Six 第六单元

第十一课： 爱好
第十二课： 我们喜欢踢球

教学目标：Objectives
❶ 拼音：zh ch sh r
❷ 句型：……喜欢……

生词：New Words
听音乐 · 唱歌 · 玩游戏 · 踢球 · 读书 · 跳舞 · 看电视

语言点：Language Point
动词短语作宾语

日常用语：Daily Expressions
❶ A：我的生日是一月一号。
B：我的生日是五月十号。
❷ 生日快乐！

汉字：Chinese Characters
风 飞

活动：Activity
制作招贴画

Introduction 导入

❶ 教师准备一些动物和场所的词语卡片。上课时，教师先做示范：把一张动物卡片和一张词语卡片叠放到一起，如“狗”和“花园”，然后拉长声调说：“狗在花园”（“在”要重读）。学生跟读。随后教师分别把“狗”和“花园”的卡片藏到身后，引导学生说出完整的句子。以此复习前一个单元学习的内容。

❷ 教师准备本课的词语卡片，打乱顺序粘贴在黑板上。教师用汉语或者英语问学生：“你们的爱好是什么？”学生依次到黑板前指卡片。如一个学生到黑板前指“听音乐”的卡片，教师就用夸张的语气大声说：“哦，××喜欢听音乐。太好了！”所有的学生都得到练习以后，教师指卡片，领读，学生跟读。最后，教师可以组织两个简单的课堂活动：（1）教师表演动作，如“听音乐”，学生说出词语；（2）一个学生到教室前边，教师背对着他，任意举起一张词语卡片，全班同学读出词语，前边的学生根据词语做动作。

❶ The teacher prepares some cards of animals and places. When the class starts, the teacher does the demonstration first. He puts a card of animal and a card of place together, for example, “狗” and “花园”, and then elongates his voice and says: “狗在花园。” (“在” should be stressed.) The students follow him. Then the teacher hides the cards with “狗” and “花园” behind his back, guiding the students to speak the complete sentence in order to review the contents in the previous unit.

❷ The teacher prepares the word cards for the lesson. Stick them on the board out of order. The teacher uses Chinese or English to ask the students: “你们的爱好是什么？(What are your hobbies?)” The students come to the board in turn to point at the cards. For example, a student comes to the board and points at the card of “听音乐”. The teacher uses the exaggerated voice to say loudly: “哦，××喜欢听音乐。太好了！” After all of the students have chances to practice, the teacher then points at the card, leads in reading, and the students follow him. Finally, the teacher can organize two simple class activities: 1) The teacher makes gestures, for example, “听音乐”, the students then speak the words; 2) A student comes to the front of the classroom. The teacher stands with his back facing the student, then he raises a card at random. All the students read out the words while the student in the front makes gestures according to the words read by them.

第11课 爱好 ài hǎo

Let's read 读一读

Zh zh zhōng

Ch ch chuán

Sh sh shù

R r rì

76

Notes

Hobbies 爱好 11

Let's read 读一读

❶ 学习声母zh、ch、sh、r的读音。

❷ 学习zh、ch、sh、r与韵母的拼合。

❶ Learn the pronunciations of the initials zh, ch, sh, and r.

❷ Learn the combination of the initials zh, ch, sh, r and the finals.

A Exercise 练一练

Listen and place a √ mark on the *pinyin* you hear. 听录音，在听到的拼音前面画√。

KEY · · 答案

① chá ② sì ③ zuǐ ④ sān ⑤ shí ⑥ shǒu

B Activity 课堂活动

With four students in a group, each student throws the ball once and says quickly the name of the picture. The group that throws and reads all four pictures with less time wins the game. 四个小朋友一组，每人扔一次球，并快速读出相应的拼音。用最短时间读完四幅图的小组获胜。

准备材料 ▶▶ 小皮球

方法 ▶▶ 教师上课前将学生用书77页"读一读"中的四幅插图画在黑板上，或者先画在白纸上，然后再粘贴在黑板上。上课时，教师按照第77页的要求做游戏。四个学生一组，每人对着黑板上的图画扔一次小球，同时用汉语说出小球投中的图画的名称，直到四幅图画都被投中并正确读出名称。教师计时，完成时间最短的小组获胜。

活动扩展 ▶▶ 学生用书第1～10课"读一读"中的图画都可以加进来，以提高游戏的难度，同时复习以前学过的拼音。

MATERIALS NEEDED ▶▶ a small leather ball

METHOD ▶▶ The teacher draws the four insert pictures in the *Let's read* section on page 77 on the Student Book on the board before the class, or draws them on the pieces of the white paper first and then sticks them onto the board. When the class starts, the teacher does the game after the directions on page 77. Four students are in a group. Each throws a small ball at the picture on the board, and says the names of the picture hit by the small ball in Chinese till all the four pictures are hit and their names said out correctly. The teacher keeps the time. The group that finishes in the shortest time wins in the end.

EXPANDED ACTIVITY ▶▶ The teacher can include all the pictures in the section *Let's read* from lesson 1-10 in the Student Book in order to increase the difficulty level, and review the *pinyin* learned before.

Chinese XP

Exercise 练一练 A

- Listen and place a √ mark on the *pinyin* you hear. 听录音，在听到的拼音前面画√。

①  • chá • cá

② 4 • sì • shì

③  • zhuǐ • zuǐ

④ 3 • shān • sān

⑤ 10 • sí • shí

⑥ 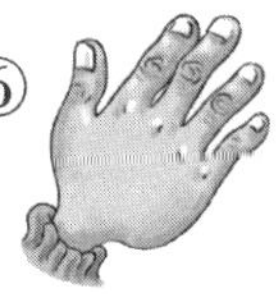 • sǒu • shǒu

Activity 课堂活动 B

- With four students in a group, each student throws the ball once and says quickly the name of the picture. The group that throws and reads all four pictures with less time wins the game. 四个小朋友一组，每人扔一次球，并快速读出相应的拼音。用最短时间读完四幅图的小组获胜。

A Let's recognize 认一认

这部分是本课学习的词语，教学方法参见本书的“使用说明”。

This section teaches the words in the lesson. Refer to the *Teacher Manual* for the teaching method.

SUPPLEMENTARY WORDS[补充生词]

打篮球 play basketball | 打棒球 play baseball | 打橄榄球 play football |
dǎ lánqiú dǎ bàngqiú dǎ gǎnlǎnqiú

玩滑板 skateboard | 轮滑 roller skate | 跑步 jog | 画画儿 draw |
wán huábǎn lúnhuá pǎobù huàhuàr

弹钢琴 play the piano | 游泳 swim
tán gāngqín yóuyǒng

B Exercises 练一练

1. Listen, number the pictures, and then match. 听录音，填序号，并连线。

KEY · · 答案

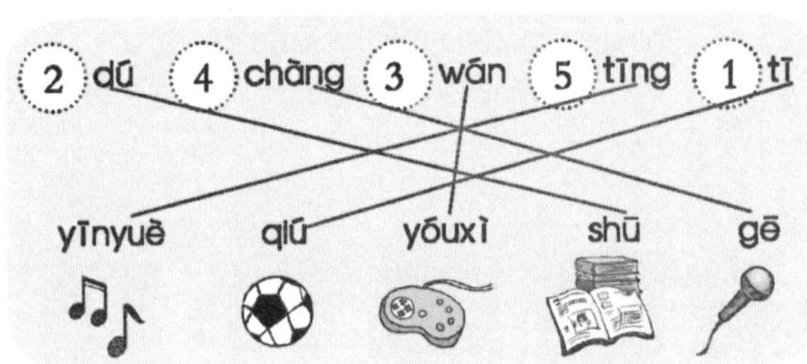

录音文本：
1. tīqiú
2. dúshū
3. wán yóuxì
4. chànggē
5. tīng yīnyuè

2. Find and write. 找一找，写一写。

KEY · · 答案

11

Let's recognize 认一认

A

听音乐
tīng yīnyuè
listen to music

唱歌
chànggē
sing

玩游戏
wán yóuxì
play games

踢球
tīqiú
play football

读书
dúshū
read

跳舞
tiàowǔ
dance

看电视
kàn diànshì
watch TV

78

Exercises 练一练

B

1 Listen, number the pictures, and then match. 听录音，填序号，并连线。

dú chàng wán tīng tī

yīnyuè qiú yóuxì shū gē

2 Find and write. 找一找，写一写。

t___ w___ d___ sh___

11 Hobbies

79

Notes

Activity 课堂活动

With two students in a group, one reads the words under the picture and states the color of the words, the other colors the paper hats in the correct pictures with the colors for the words. 两个小朋友一组，一人读出下边的词语，并说出汉字的颜色，另一人根据人物动作为图中人物的帽子涂上与词语相同的颜色。

准备材料 彩笔

方法 按照学生用书第80页的要求做练习。两个学生一组，学生A读出图下方的词语，同时说出汉字的颜色，如"跳舞—红色"，学生B根据同伴的提示为图中正在跳舞的那个人的帽子涂上红色。全部涂完后，两人对换角色，学生B读出词语，学生A涂色。学生全部完成后，教师检查结果，正确率最高的小组获胜。

MATERIALS NEEDED color pens

METHOD Practice after the directions on page 80 in the Student Book. Two students are in a group. Student A reads out the words under the picture, and says out the color in Chinese at the same time. For example, "跳舞—红色". Student B then paints the dancer's hat with the red color in the picture according to the prompts by his fellow student. After coloring all the parts in the picture, the two switch roles. This time Student B reads out the words, Student A colors. After they are all done, the teacher checks the results. The group with the highest correct percentage wins in the end.

Let's say 说一说

教学方法参见本书的"使用说明"。

替换词语 对话中的日期可以替换，请学生们分别介绍一下自己的生日。

Refer to the *Teacher Manual* for the teaching method in the book.

SUBSTITUTE WORDS The dates in the dialogue can be substituted. Invite the students to introduce their birthdays respectively.

11
A
Activity 课堂活动
With two students in a group, one reads the words under the picture and states the color of the words, the other colors the paper hats in the correct pictures with the colors for the words. 两个小朋友一组，一人读出下边的词语，并说出汉字的颜色，另一人根据人物动作为图中人物的帽子涂上与词语相同的颜色。
跳舞 tiàowǔ
玩游戏 wán yóuxì
踢球 tīqiú
听音乐 tīng yīnyuè
读书 dúshū
80

Let's say 说一说
B
1 我的生日是一月一号。
Wǒ de shēngrì shì yī yuè yī hào.
My birthday is January 1st.
2 我的生日是五月十号。
Wǒ de shēngrì shì wǔ yuè shí hào.
My birthday is May 10th.
1月1号
11
Hobbies
生日快乐！
Shēngrì kuàilè!
Happy birthday !
81

Notes

Supplementary activities 补充活动

1. Listen to the sounds and change the initials 听音改读

方法 学生分为两大组。教师说几组分别包含有声母zh、ch、sh的音节，每组派一个学生将其改读为声母为z、c、s而韵母和声调不变的音节，例如，教师说“zhāng”，学生改读为“zāng”。改读正确加1分，改读错误不加分。教师计分。得分最高的小组获胜。如果时间允许，也可以教师说声母为z、c、s的音节，学生将其改为声母为zh、ch、sh的音节。

参考读音 zhī—zī chī—cī shī—sī zhōu—zōu chōu—cōu shōu—sōu zhāng—zāng chuǎn—cuǎn shǎng—sǎng zhōng—zōng chóng—cóng shuì—suì

METHOD Divide the students into two big groups. The teacher says several groups of syllables including the initials zh, ch, and sh. Each group designates one student to change them into the syllables with z, c, and s as their initials, while keeping the same finals and tones. For example, the teacher says “zhang”, the student then changes into “zang”. The correct change earns one point while the incorrect one gets no point. The teacher keeps the points. The group with the higher point wins in the end. If time permits, the teacher can say the syllables with z, c, and s as the initials the student then changes them into the syllables with zh, ch, and sh.

REFERENCE PINYIN See the Chinese version on the left.

2. Connect the words into lines 连词成线

准备材料 活动页（见附页11.2）

方法 复印足够数量的活动页，发给每个学生一份。教师说词语，学生在听到的词语上标序号，同时画×。先把五个词语连成一条直线或者斜线的学生举手示意，教师检查结果，如果序号正确，那么这个学生会先得到一个奖励。教师继续说词语，直到全班的学生都至少将五个词语连成一条直线或者斜线。连出最多直线或者斜线的学生获胜。

MATERIALS NEEDED Activity Page (See attachment 11.2)

METHOD Make enough copies of the Activity Page. Give a copy to each student. The teacher says the words. The students mark the serial numbers on the words heard, and make a tick at the same time. The student who first makes the five words into a linear line or a slant one raises his hand to draw attention from the teacher, who then checks his work. If the serial number is correct, then the student can get a prize. The teacher continues

练习词语 ➡ 1. 听音乐 2. 唱歌 3. 看电视 4. 听音乐 5. 踢球 6. 玩游戏 7. 跳舞 8. 玩游戏 9. 踢球 10. 唱歌 11. 听音乐 12. 读书 13. 唱歌 14. 听音乐 15. 读书 16. 唱歌 17. 看电视 18. 跳舞 19. 踢球 20. 玩游戏

参考答案 ➡ 可以连出一条斜线和五条直线

to say the words till all the students in the class have been able to connect at least one linear line or a slant line with these five words. The student who connects the most linear lines or the slant lines wins in the end.

PRACTICE WORDS ➡ See the Chinese version on the left.

ANSWER ➡ Five linear lines and one slant line can be made.

3. Who has the birthday on the same day as someone else? 谁和谁的生日是同一天？

准备材料 ➡ 活动页（见附页11.3）

方法 ➡ 复印活动页。学生两人一组，学生A拿A图，学生B拿B图，互相不能看对方的图。学生A告诉对方A图上某人的生日是几月几号，学生B在B图上找出是否有相同的日期，如果有，用彩笔将人名涂上。对照完所有人的生日以后，每组学生统计一下，A图和B图中一共有几个人的生日是在同一天。做得又快又好的小组将得到一个小奖励。

句型示例 ➡ ××的生日是×月×号。

参考答案 ➡ 有五个人的生日相同

MATERIALS NEEDED ➡ Activity Page (See attachment 11.3)

METHOD ➡ Make copies of the Activity Page. Two students are in a group. Student A holds Picture A and Student B holds Picture B. They can't see the other's picture. Student A tells Student B the birthday date on Picture A; Student B then looks at Picture B to see if it has the same date on it. If it has, then use the color pen to paint the person's name on it. After checking everyone's birthday each group makes a calculation on how many people have birthdays on the same day on both Picture A and Picture B. The group that does it faster and better gets a small prize.

EXAMPLE ➡ See the Chinese version on the left.

ANSWER ➡ Five persons have the same date.

12 We like to play football 我们喜欢踢球

A Let's learn 学一学

❶ 本课的语言点是动词短语作宾语。与英语不同的是，汉语里的动词短语作宾语，动词没有形式上的变化，直接放在谓语动词的后边即可，例如“我喜欢跳舞”。

❷ 教师将本课的词语卡片贴在黑板上，指着卡片说：“他喜欢——”（“喜欢”要重读），引导学生将句子补充完整：“他喜欢听音乐”。教师领读几次，直到学生熟悉地掌握这个句型。随后教师问学生：“你们谁喜欢听音乐？”学生举手回答，教师重复：“哦，××喜欢听音乐。太棒了！”用这种方法继续练习黑板上的所有词语。

❸ 教师让学生打开书，看图，听录音，跟读课本中的句子。这部分配有替换词语，可以用来进行替换练习。练习之前教师把句型“……喜欢……”写在黑板上，然后指着替换部分的第一幅图做示范：一边做出“听音乐”的动作一边用第一人称模仿男孩子的声音说：“我喜欢听音乐”，然后换一个位置，用第三人称以教师的身份说：“哦，他喜欢听音乐”，让学生跟着模仿。随后教师任意指一幅图，找几个学生试着说出句子。学生说完后，教师说一遍正确的句子，全班学生跟读。如果时间允许，教师可以组织一个小游戏：两个学

❶ This lesson's language point is on the verbal phrase functioning as object, which has no change in form; it follows the verb directly. For example, “我喜欢跳舞”. This differs from English.

❷ The teacher sticks the word cards in the lesson on the board, then points at the cards and says: “他喜欢——” (“喜欢” should be stressed) to guide the students to complete the sentence: “他喜欢听音乐”. The teacher leads in reading for several times till the students get familiar with this sentence pattern. Then the teacher asks the students: “谁喜欢听音乐?” They raise their hands to answer the question. The teacher repeats: “哦，××喜欢听音乐。太棒了！” Use this method to continue to practice all the words on the board.

❸ The teacher asks the students to open their looks, look at the picture, listen to the recording, and follow reading the sentences in the lesson. This section is provided with the substitute words, which can be used in substitution drill. Before the exercise, the teacher writes down the sentence pattern “……喜欢……” on the board, then points at the first picture in the substitution section, the teacher starts to do the demonstration.

第12课 我们喜欢踢球

wǒ men xǐ huan tī qiú

Let's learn 学一学

82

生一组，教师模仿图中的人物说句子，如“我喜欢跳舞”，学生指出相应的图片，先指对的学生获胜。

While making the gesture “听音乐” the teacher uses the first person pronoun imitating a boy and says: “我喜欢听音乐”. Then changing into another position, the teacher says in the third person pronoun as a teacher and says: “哦，他喜欢听音乐”. Have the students imitate him. Then the teacher points at a picture at random and asks several students to try to say the sentences. After the students are done with speaking, the teacher says the correct sentence once and has the whole class follow him. If time permits, the teacher can organize a little game: two students are in a group, the teacher imitates the person in the picture to say the sentences, for example, “我喜欢跳舞”. The students point at the corresponding picture. The student who first identifies the picture correctly wins.

TEXT TRANSLATION[课文译文]

我们喜欢踢球。We like to play soccer.

B

PATTERN'S SUBSTITUTE[句型替换]

我/他喜欢听音乐。 我/他喜欢玩游戏。
我/她喜欢唱歌。 我/她喜欢看电视。
我/她喜欢跳舞。 我/她喜欢读书。

Let's try 试一试

B

______ 喜欢 ______。

xǐhuan

tīng yīnyuè

wán yóuxì

chànggē

kàn diànshì

tiàowǔ

dúshū

A Look and sing 看一看，唱一唱

歌曲的学习方法参见本书的“使用说明”。

活动方法 ➡ 学生们学会歌曲以后，教师组织课堂活动。学生站成一圈，教师先做示范：教师做一个动作，如“踢球”，同时说：“球—踢球”，学生模仿动作，同时跟读词语。随后教师领着学生一边做动作一起唱歌：“球球球球，踢球。他喜欢踢球……”用这种方法练习本课学习的所有词语。教师可以找一个或几个学生分别做动作，其他学生唱歌；或者找两个学生到教室前边，教师背着他们举卡片，全班学生根据卡片上的词语唱歌，前边两个学生做动作。

歌曲文本 ➡ 球球球球，踢球。他喜欢踢球。（重复）音乐音乐，听音乐。他喜欢听音乐。（重复）

Refer to the *Teacher Manual* for the method for learning the song in the book.

METHOD ➡ After the students have learned the song, the teacher organizes the class activity: the students stand in a circle, the teacher then starts to do the demonstration: the teacher makes gestures, for example, “踢球”, and says at the same time: “球—踢球”, the students imitate the action, and follow the teacher in reading the words. After that, the teacher leads the students in making movements and they sing simultaneously: “球球球球，踢球。他喜欢踢球……” Use this method to practice all the words in the lesson. The teacher can find one or several students to make movements while the other students sing; or ask two students to come to the front. The teacher raises the cards with his back facing the students. The whole class sings the song according to the words on the card. The two students in the front make movements.

THE SONG SCRIPT ➡ Ball ball ball ball, play the soccer. He likes to play the soccer.(Repeat) Music music, listen to the music. He likes to listen to the music. (Repeat)

B Sentence patterns 学句型

Read the patterns aloud, and then look at the pictures and compose sentences with “喜欢”. 大声朗读句型，然后看图用“喜欢”造句。

❶ 这部分是句型总结与复习。教师领学生反复大声朗读句型框里的句型，直到学生可以流利地读出句型框里的句子。

❶ This section is the summary of the sentence patterns and the reviews. The teacher leads the students in reading out loud the sentence

12

Look and sing 看一看，唱一唱

A

Qiú qiú qiú qiú, tīqiú.
Tā xǐhuan tīqiú.
Qiú qiú qiú qiú, tīqiú.
Tā xǐhuan tīqiú.

Yīnyuè yīnyuè, tīng yīnyuè.
Tā xǐhuan tīng yīnyuè.
Yīnyuè yīnyuè, tīng yīnyuè.
Tā xǐhuan tīng yīnyuè.

84

Sentence patterns 学句型

B

- Read the patterns aloud, and then look at the pictures and compose sentences with “喜欢”. 大声朗读句型，然后看图用“喜欢”造句。

我 wǒ / 我们 wǒmen — 喜欢 xǐhuan — 唱歌 chànggē / 跳舞 tiàowǔ

12 We like to play football

85

Notes

❷ 学生看图，用“……喜欢……”造句，可以用拼音或者汉字写出答案，教师个别指导并给出成绩。

patterns in the box till the students can read out them fluently.

❷ The students look at the picture, using “……喜欢……” to make up sentences. They can use either *pinyin* or the characters to write out the answers. The teacher supervises individually and gives out grades.

KEY · · 答案

我/她喜欢跳舞。 我/他喜欢读书。 我/她喜欢唱歌。 我/他喜欢踢球。

A Interesting characters 趣味汉字

本课学习的汉字是“风”和“飞”，要求学生掌握这两个字的正确写法。汉字的教学方法参见本书的“使用说明”。

This lesson teaches the characters “风” and “飞”. The students are required to master the correct way of writing these two characters. Refer to the *Teacher Manual* for the teaching method in the book.

B Let's do it 做一做

Make a poster: My hobbies 做招贴画：我的爱好

准备材料 ▶▶ 铅笔、彩笔、剪刀、胶棒、照片

方法 ▶▶ 教师事先让学生准备一张自己的近照和几张做活动的照片。上课时，学生在课本或者另一张白纸上做一个展现自己爱好的招贴画。除了贴上自己的近照，写上自己的名字以外，其他部分学生可以自由发挥，既可以贴照片，也可以画图，目的在于用招贴画向大家介绍自己的爱好。如果学生汉语水平较高，教师可以要求学生在招贴画上写出与照片或者图画相符的句子，如“我喜欢跳舞。”制作完成后，教师可以在学

MATERIALS NEEDED ▶▶ pencils, color pens, scissors, glue sticks, and photos.

METHOD ▶▶ The teacher asks the student to have a recent photo of him and a couple of photos for the activity ready before the class. Once in class, the students make a self introduction poster of their liking on the textbook or on a piece of paper. Besides sticking his recent photo and writing his name on the poster, the students can do the rest parts creatively. They can both stick their photos and draw pictures. The purpose is to introduce their hobbies to the

12

Interesting characters 趣味汉字

A

wind

风

fēng

风 风 风 风

fly

飞

fēi

飞 飞 飞 飞

86

Let's do it 做一做

B

- Make a poster : My hobbies 做招贴画：我的爱好

my photo

姓名：________

name

12 We like to play football

87

Notes

生的作品上分别印上一个奖励的小印章，也可以跟学生一起做一期招贴画的墙报。

public via the picture poster. If the students are advanced with Chinese, the teacher can ask them to write out the sentences matching the photos or the pictures on the poster, for example, "我喜欢跳舞。" Upon drawing the picture, the teacher can put a small reward stamp on it and also can do the wall poster together with the students.

Supplementary activities 补充活动

1. Card game 卡片游戏

准备材料▶▶ 活动页（见附页12.1）

方法▶▶ 复印活动页，并将活动页上的小图剪下来，作为小卡片发给学生。将学生分为4～5人一组，每组发两套小卡片，然后选一个汉语比较好的学生做组长。教师把小卡片正面朝下摆放在小组的桌子上。每个学生每次只能翻开一张卡片，如果能用汉语说出卡片上动作的名称，就可以留下这张小卡片，否则就要将卡片重新放回到桌子上。每组的组长做裁判，教师巡视指导。游戏完成后，每组得到最多卡片的学生获胜。

MATERIALS NEEDED▶▶ Activity Page (See attachment 12.1)

METHOD▶▶ Make copies of the Activity Page. Cut out the small pictures on the Activity Page and then give them back to the students in the form of the small cards. Divide the students into groups of 4-5 and give two sets of small cards to each group. Then select a student who speaks better Chinese as the group leader. The teacher puts the little cards face up on the desktop where the group sits around. Each student can only turn over one card each time. If he can speak the names of the actions on the card, he can keep the card. Otherwise, he will have to put back the card on the desktop. The group leader acts like a judge. The teacher supervises and gives directions. The group that gets the most cards wins in the end.

2. Similar hobbies 相同的爱好

准备材料▶▶ 活动页（见附页12.2）

MATERIALS NEEDED▶▶ Activity Page (See attachment 12.2)

方法 ➧ 复印活动页，学生两人一组，学生A拿A图，学生B拿B图，互相不能看对方的图。学生A告诉对方A图上某人的爱好，同时说出序号，如“1.弟弟喜欢玩游戏”，学生B在B图上找出爱好相同的那个人，并在图下写出相同的序号。完成后，教师检查结果，完全做对的小组可以得到一个小奖励。

参考句型 ➧ ××喜欢……

METHOD ➧ Make copies of the Activity Page. Two students are in a group. Student A holds Picture A and the Student B holds Picture B. They can't see the other's picture. Student A tells Student B someone's hobby in Picture B, for example, “1.弟弟喜欢玩游戏”. Student B looks for the person on Picture B, who shares the similar hobbies. Then write the same number under the small picture. Upon completion, the group that has done everything correctly may get a small prize.

SENTENCE PATTERN ➧ See the Chinese version on the left.

3. Connect the words into sentences 连词成句

准备材料 ➧ 剪刀、活动页（见附页12.3）

方法 ➧ 复印足够数量的活动页，发给每个学生一份。学生先用剪刀把活动页上的词语剪下来，然后在空白的方格中写上自己的家人或者朋友的名字，然后将这些词语排列成五个句子。看看谁做得又快又好。

MATERIALS NEEDED ➧ scissors, Activity Page (See attachment 12.3)

METHOD ➧ Make enough copies of the Activity Page. Give each student a copy. The students use the scissors to cut out the words on the Activity Page and then write down his family members' or his friends' names in the blank grids. Then arrange these words into five sentences. See who can finish it fast and best.

A game 小游戏

准备材料 ➧ 一分的硬币或者色子

方法 ➧ 按照学生用书第88页的要求做游戏。学生四人一组，围坐在一起，将课本打开翻到88页，放在桌子上边，每人投掷一次硬币，然后用硬币投中的词语造句，如“我喜欢唱歌”，同时做一个相应的动作。教师巡视，个别指导。

MATERIALS NEEDED ➧ a penny coin or a dice

METHOD ➧ Do the game according to the directions on page 88 in the Student Book. Put four students in a group. Have them sit in a circle. Open the Student Book and turn to page 88. Put it on the table. Each student throws a coin and then uses the word which the coin hits to make up a sentence, i.e., “我喜欢唱歌”, and makes a corresponding move at the same time. The teacher walks around giving individual guidance.

Story time 故事会

教学方法参见本书的“使用说明”。

故事文本 ➧ 每人都有自己的爱好。丁丁问明明有什么爱好，明明说：“我喜欢画画儿。”丁丁问兰兰有什么爱好，兰兰说：“我喜欢读书。”丁丁有什么爱好呢？丁丁说：“我喜欢睡觉。”“我喜欢吃东西。”期末考试的成绩出来了，兰兰得了A，明明得了B，爱睡觉和爱吃东西的丁丁只得了D。丁丁很难过，他说：“我不喜欢D。”丁丁下决心要培养一些更好的爱好了。

Refer to the *Teacher Manual* for the teaching method in the book.

STORY TEXT ➧ Everyone has his own hobby. Dingding asks Mingming what hobby he has. Mingming says: “我喜欢画画儿。” Dingding asks Lanlan what hobby she has. Lanlan says: “我喜欢读书。” What hobby does Dingding have? Dingding says: “我喜欢睡觉。”“我喜欢吃东西。” The grade for the final exam has come out. Lanlan gets an A, Mingming gets a B. The sleep and food liking Dingding has got merely a D. Dingding is very sad. He says: “我不喜欢D。” He is determined to foster some better hobbies.

Review 6 (复习6)

A

1 A game 小游戏

- Throw a coin. Compose a sentence with the word that the coin hits, and then do an action according to the meaning of the sentence. 投掷硬币，用硬币投中的词语造句，然后根据句子的意思做一个动作。

tīqiú	wán yóuxì	tīng yīnyuè	tīqiú
tīng yīnyuè	chànggē	tiàowǔ	dǎzì
wán yóuxì	kàn diànshì	dúshū	tīqiú
tiàowǔ	dúshū	tīqiú	tiàowǔ
chànggē	tīng yīnyuè	chànggē	wán yóuxì

88

B

2 Story time 故事会

89

Notes

TRANSLATION[译文] ➡ 图1：我喜欢画画儿。I like to draw pictures.

图2：我喜欢读书。I like to read books.

图3：我喜欢睡觉。I like to sleep.

我喜欢吃东西。I like to eat.

图4：我不喜欢D。I do not like mark D.

Unit Seven 第七单元

第十三课：能力
第十四课：我会打字

教学目标： Objectives
❶ 拼音：y w
❷ 句型：……会……

生词： New Words
打字 · 画画儿 · 弹钢琴 · 做饭 · 打篮球 · 游泳 · 会

语言点： Language Point
"会"的用法

日常用语： Daily Expressions
A：喂！你好！
B：你好！请问杰克在吗？
A：我就是。

汉字： Chinese Characters
马 书

活动： Activity
制作海报：我的朋友

Introduction 导入

❶ 教师利用前一单元学生制作的"爱好"招贴画进行复习。教师指着招贴画上的照片和图片用汉语或英语问学生："他是谁？""他的爱好是什么？"学生回答后，教师重复："对！他是××。他喜欢踢球。"以此复习前一单元的内容。

❷ 教师准备本课的词语卡片，打乱顺序贴在黑板上。教师先做示范：先指卡片，然后做动作，同时说句字，如："打字。老师会打字。"接着用汉语或者英语问学生："你们会做什么？"学生依次到黑板前指卡片。如一个学生到黑板前指"弹钢琴"的卡片，教师就用夸张的语气大声说："哦，××会弹钢琴。他真棒！"所有的学生都得到练习以后，教师指卡片，领读，学生跟读。最后，教师可以组织两个简单的课堂活动：（1）教师表演动作，如"弹钢琴"，学生说出词语；（2）一个学生到教室前边，教师背对着他，任意举起一张词语卡片，全班同学读出词语，前边的学生根据词语做动作。

❶ The teacher takes advantage of the picture poster on *hobbies* in the previous unit. He points at the photos and the pictures on the poster and asks the students "他是谁？ (Who is he?)" "他的爱好是什么？(What is his hobby?)" After the students have answered these questions, the teacher repeats:"对！他是××。他喜欢踢球。" This class activity is used to review the contents in the previous unit.

❷ After the teacher has prepared the word cards for the lesson, he sticks them out of order on the board. The teacher starts to do the demonstration first. He makes gestures and says the sentences while pointing at the cards:"打字。老师会打字。" Then he asks the students either in Chinese or English:"你们会做什么？(What can you do?)" The students come to the board to point at the cards in turn. For example, a student points at a card showing "弹钢琴" The teacher then uses the exaggerated voice to say loudly:"哦，××会弹钢琴。他真棒！" After all the students get a chance to practice, the teacher points at the card, leads in reading, and the students follow him. By the end of class, the teacher can organize two simple class activities: (1) the teacher acts out, for example,"弹钢琴", then the students speak out the words; (2) one student comes to the front, the teacher turns his back to him, raises a card at random, the whole class reads out the word on the card while the student in the front makes gestures according to the word he has heard.

第13课 能力
nēng lì

Let's read 读一读

A

Y y

yún

yuè

W w

wǔ

5

wǎn

90

Notes

Ability 能力 13

A

Let's read 读一读

❶ 学习声母 y、w 的读音。

❷ 学习 y、w 与韵母的拼合。

❶ Learn the pronunciations of the initials y and w.

❷ Learn the combination of the initials y, w and the finals.

A Exercise 练一练

Listen and color the pinyin you hear. 听录音，为你听到的拼音涂上颜色。

KEY · · 答案

录音文本：yī yí yǐ wū wú

B Activity 课堂活动

With two students in a group, each student chooses a picture at random, draws it and writes the pinyin. Then passes the picture to his/her partner. The partner takes the picture, runs quickly to the teacher and reads the *pinyin*. 两个小朋友一组，每人任意选一幅图画出来，写出拼音，然后把图传给同伴。同伴拿着图快速跑到老师身边，读出图上的拼音。

方法 教师提前把学生用书第90页的四幅图画在黑板上，或者先画在纸上，然后贴在黑板上。两个学生一组，每人任选黑板上的一幅图，在白纸上画出来，并写出拼音或者汉字。两个人都完成后，互相交换图画，然后分别拿着同伴的图画快速跑到教师面前，大声读出图上的拼音或汉字。教师检查，正确的给予鼓励或者奖励，错误的由教师帮忙改正过来。

活动扩展 学生将自己画的图涂上颜色，然后跟教师一起做一期墙报。

METHOD The teacher draws the four pictures on page 90 in the Student Book on the board beforehand, or draws them first on the pieces of white paper, and then sticks them on the board. Two students are in a group. Each chooses a picture on the board at random, draws them on the pieces of the white paper and writes out either in *pinyin* or the characters. After the two have finished they switch the pictures. Then they run to the teacher holding the picture of the other's, read out the *pinyin* loudly. The teacher checks their answers. If correct, the teacher gives them encouragement or prizes; if not, the teacher corrects the mistakes.

EXPANDED ACTIVITY Students paint their drawings with colors, and then make a wall bulletin together with the teacher.

Exercise 练一练 A

- Listen and color the *pinyin* you hear. 听录音，为你听到的拼音涂上颜色。

yī	yí	yǐ	yì
wū	wú	wǔ	wù

Activity 课堂活动 B

- With two students in a group, each student chooses a picture at random, draws it and writes the *pinyin*. Then passes the picture to his/her partner. The partner takes the picture, runs quickly to the teacher and reads the *pinyin*. 两个小朋友一组，每人任意选一幅图画出来，写出拼音，然后把图传给同伴。同伴拿着图快速跑到老师身边，读出图上的拼音。

A Let's recognize 认一认

这部分是本课学习的词语，教学方法参见本书的“使用说明”。

This section teaches the words in the lesson. Refer to the *Teacher Manual* for the teaching method in the book.

SUPPLEMENTARY WORDS[补充生词]

开车 drive a car | 打网球 play tennis | 打棒球 play baseball |
kāichē　dǎ wǎngqiú　dǎ bàngqiú

打橄榄球 play football | 骑自行车 ride on a bicycle |
dǎ gǎnlǎnqiú　qí zìxíngchē

骑马 ride on a horse | 说汉语 speak Chinese
qímǎ　shuō hànyǔ

B Exercises 练一练

1. Listen, number the *pinyin*, and then match. 听录音，填序号，然后连线。

KEY · · 答案

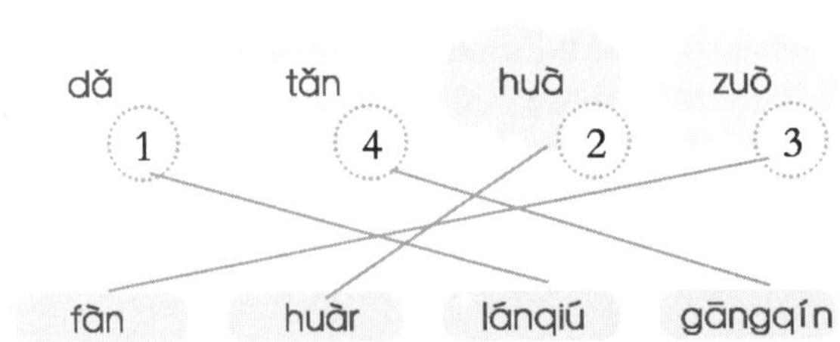

录音文本：
1. dǎ lánqiú
2. huàhuàr
3. zuòfàn
4. tán gāngqín

2. Listen and place a √ mark for the correct picture. 听录音，在正确的图片下边画√。

KEY · · 答案

录音文本：
1. 弹钢琴
2. 游泳
3. 打篮球
4. 画画儿

13

Let's recognize 认一认

A

打字
dǎzì
type

画画儿
huà huàr
paint

弹钢琴
tán gāngqín
play the piano

做饭
zuòfàn
cook

打篮球
dǎ lánqiú
play basketball

游泳
yóuyǒng
swim

会 huì can, be able to

92

B

Exercises 练一练

1 Listen, number the *pinyin*, and then match. 听录音，填序号，然后连线

dǎ tán huà zuò

fàn huàr lánqiú gāngqín

2 Listen and place a √ mark for the correct picture. 听录音，在正确的图片下边画√。

①

②

③

④

13 Ability

93

Notes

Activity 课堂活动

With two students in a group, look at the small picture in the grid below for 10 seconds. Then one student covers one square with a small paper board. The other student guesses what the person in the covered square is doing. Then, the first student removes the small paper board and states the answer. (see Page 126 at the back of the book for the paper board.) 两个小朋友一组，用10秒钟的时间看一遍下面表格里的小图，然后用纸板把表格盖上。一人猜一猜每个小格里的人在做什么，另一人揭开小纸板，说出答案。（纸板见书后第126页）

方法 教师指导学生将学生用书第126页的纸板剪下来，沿白色虚线将纸剪开，注意每个部分都不要剪断，最后剪成九个可以向上掀开的小窗口的样子就可以了。纸板做好后，按照学生用书第94页的要求做游戏。教师先领读两遍九幅插图中表现的词语，然后两个学生一组，教师计时，让学生用10秒钟的时间看图，尽可能记下来图中每个小格里的内容。10秒钟以后，学生A用板纸将整幅图盖上，学生B猜出每个小格里的人在做什么，可以用汉语说出词语，如“打篮球”，也可以做动作表示。每猜完一个，学生A就揭开板纸上的那个小窗口，检查结果是否正确。学生B猜完全部九个小格里的内容后，轮换角色，由学生A来猜词，学生B检查。

活动扩展 教师也可以组织全班活动。教师在黑板上画一个三行三列的表格，每个小格里写上1～9的数字。教师先给学生们10秒钟的时间看课本上的大图，然后合上课本，一起看黑板上的表格。教师任指一个小格，或者说出一个数字，如“9”，学生举手抢答课本上同样位置的那个小格里的人在做什么，

METHOD The teacher directs the students to cut out the paper board from page 126 on the Student Book. Cut along the white dotted lines, making sure that all of the parts are connected. In the end, nine small windows that can't be opened upward emerge. After that, start a game after the directions on page 94 in the Student Book. The teacher leads in reading the words on the nine pictures twice. Then put two students in a group. The teacher keeps the time. Have the students look at the picture in ten seconds, trying to remember the contents in each square in the pictures. After ten seconds, Student A covers the whole picture with a piece of paper board, Student B guesses what the people are doing in each square. He can speak in Chinese, for example, “打篮球”. He can also make gestures to express the meaning of the words. After each guess, Student A opens the window on each paper board to verify if the answer is correct. After Student B has guessed all the contents of the nine squares, they switch the roles. This time, Student A guesses the words and Student B

13

Activity 课堂活动

- With two students in a group, look at the small picture in the grid below for 10 seconds. Then one student covers one square with a small paper board. The other student guesses what the person in the covered square is doing. Then, the first student removes the small paper board and states the answer. (see Page 126 at the back of the book for the paper board.) 两个小朋友一组，用10秒钟的时间看一遍下面表格里的小图，然后用纸板把表格盖上。一人猜一猜每个小格里的人在做什么，另一人揭开小纸板，说出答案。（纸板见书后第126页）

如"踢球"。教师把最先答对的学生的名字写到那个小格里，直到所有九个小格的内容都被正确猜出。

参考词语 ➽ 打字、画画儿、弹钢琴、做饭、游泳、打篮球、跳舞、唱歌、踢球

checks the answers.

EXPANDED ACTIVITY ➽ The teacher can also organize the whole class activity. He draws a 3 × 3 chart on the board. Each small square is written with numbers 1-9. The teacher first gives the students ten seconds to look at the big picture on the textbook, and then has them close the books. After that, they look at the chart on the board together. The teacher points at a small square, or says a number, for example, 9; the students raise their hands to compete to answer what the people are doing in the square in the same position in the book, for example,"踢球". The teacher puts the name of the student who first answered correctly into that square. The activity continues till all the contents from the nine squares have been figured out.

WORDS FOR REFERENCE ➽ See the Chinese version.

A Let's say 说一说

教学方法参见本书的"使用说明"。

替换词语 ➽ 对话中的人名可以替换。

Refer to the *Teacher Manual* for the teaching method in the book.

SUBSTITUTE WORDS ➽ The person's name can be substituted in the dialogue.

Let's say 说一说

1
喂！你好！
Wéi！ Nǐhǎo！
Hello!
2
你好！请 问杰克在吗？
Nǐhǎo！Qǐng wèn Jiékè zài ma?
Hello! Is Jack in?
3
我就是。
Wǒ jiù shì.
This is Jack.

Supplementary activities 补充活动

1. Look and read 找一找，读一读

准备材料 活动页（见附页13.1）

方法 复印足够数量的活动页，发给每个学生一份。学生在最短的时间内找到活动页上的儿歌里有几个y，几个w，把数字写到儿歌下边的空心圆里。写完后，教师检查结果，全部数对的学生可以得到一个小奖励。最后，教师领读儿歌，凡是有y，w的地方要重读，以加深学生的印象。

参考答案 y（10个）w（7个）

MATERIALS NEEDED Activity Page (See attachment 13.1)

METHOD Make enough copies of the Activity Page. Give each student a copy. Have the students find how many y, and w in the children's song on the Activity Page in the shortest time possible. Write the numbers in the blank circles under the children's song. After that, the teacher checks the results. The students who are perfect in the task may get a small prize. In the end, the teacher leads in reading the children's song. Stress the places where y and w appear to deepen the students' impression.

2. Guess the words 猜词语

准备材料 若干词语卡片

方法 教师准备一些写有动词短语的卡片。学生两人一组，每组可以自己起一个名字，如"苹果组"等，教师把组名写到黑板上。教师先请一组学生走到教室前边，面对面站着，中间间隔一段距离。教师站到学生A的后边，举起一张卡片，学生B根据卡片上的词语表演动作，学生A要在10秒钟内猜出卡片上的词语是什么。超过规定时间教师就要换一张卡片。每组学生猜五张卡片，老师把每组猜对的词语数量写在黑板上，猜对最多词语的小组获胜。

参考词语 打字、画画儿、弹钢琴、

MATERIALS NEEDED some word cards

METHOD The teacher prepares some cards related with verbal phrases. Put two students into a group. Each group can make a name for the group, for example, "Apple Group", etc. The teacher puts the group names on the board, and then invites one group of students to the front. Have them stand facing each other. Keep a certain distance between the group members. The teacher stands behind Student A, raises a card; Student B makes moves according to the words on the cards. Student A has to guess out the meaning of the word

做饭、打篮球、游泳、听音乐、唱歌、玩游戏、踢球、读书、跳舞、看电视、喝水

in ten seconds. Beyond that time, the teacher will change for the next card. Each group does five cards. The teacher then writes down the correct numbers by each group on the board. The group with the most correct words wins in the end.

WORDS FOR REFERENCE ➽ See the Chinese version

3. Look for objects 找物品

准备材料 ➽ 剪刀、胶棒、活动页（见附页13.3）

方法 ➽ 复印足够数量的活动页，发给每个学生一份。学生先将图中的物品剪下来，然后粘贴在正确的圆圈里。学生完成后，教师检查，全做对的学生可以得到一个小奖励。

MATERIALS NEEDED ➽ scissors, glue sticks, Activity Page (See attachment 13.3)

METHOD ➽ Make enough copies of the Activity Page. Give each student a copy. The students cut out the objects from the picture, and then stick them in the right circles. After that, the teacher checks their works. The students who have done without any mistakes can get a small prize.

14 I can type 我会打字

A Let's learn 学一学

❶ 本课学习能愿动词“会”。“会”表示通过学习获得某种能力，它的否定形式是“不会”，表示不具备某种能力。本课句型的基本格式是“主语+会/不会+宾语”，其中宾语通常为动词短语，例如“我会游泳”，“我不会做饭”。

❷ 教师先拿出“游泳”的卡片做示范：（1）做出漂亮的游泳的动作，同时大声说“我/老师会游泳”（“会”要重读）。（2）做出在水里挣扎的动作，同时气喘吁吁地说：“我/老师不会游泳”（“不会”拉长调，重读）。教师做完示范后，拿着卡片走到每个学生面前，问“你会游泳吗？”学生回答后，教师重复句子：“哦，××会/不会游泳”。用这种方法练习本单元学习所有的动词短语。

❸ 教师可以组织两个小游戏：（1）教师把本单元的词语卡片贴在黑板上，问学生：“你们会做什么？”让学生走到黑板前，站到相应的卡片下边，然后依次说：“我会……”（2）学生分为两组，一组每次派一个学生表演动作，另一组每次派一个学生根据对方学生的动作选择正确的卡片，把卡片举起来，并读出卡片上的词语。教师做裁判，对表现好的学生给予鼓励或者奖励。

❶ This lesson teaches the auxiliary verb “会”, which expresses obtaining a skill through study. Its negative form is “不会”, expressing not possessing a skill. The basic sentence pattern is: “subject + 会/不会 + object”. Verbal phrases usually function as objects, for example, “我会游泳”, “我不会做饭”.

❷ The teacher first takes out the card “游泳” for the demonstration: (1) make beautiful swimming moves, and say loudly at the same time: “我/老师会游泳”. “会” is stressed. (2) Make struggling gestures in the water, shouts out of breath: “我/老师不会游泳”. “不会” is stressed and said longer. After the demonstration, the teacher takes the card and comes to the front of each student, asking “你会游泳吗？(Can you swim?)” After the students answer the question, the teacher repeats the sentence: “哦，××会/不会游泳”. Practice all the verbal phrases in the unit with this method.

❸ The teacher can organize two small games: (1) stick the word cards in the lesson on the board, and ask the students: “你们会做什么？(What can you do?)” Have the students come to the board, stand under the corresponding cards, and then say in turn: “我会……” (2) put the students into two groups. Each

第14课 我会打字

wǒ huì dǎ zì

Let's learn 学一学

96

❹教师让学生打开书，看图，听录音，跟读课本中的句子。这部分没有替换词语。教师让学生看课本上的大图，教师说句子，如“她会弹钢琴”，学生指图，同时重复句子。教师分别检查。

time each group chooses one student to make gestures, expressing what he can do; the other group sends a student to choose the correct cards according to the moves by the student from the other group, and then raises the card and reads out the words in the card. The teacher acts as the judge. Give encouragement or prizes to the students who have done a good job.

❹ The teacher asks the students to open their books, look at the pictures, listen to the recording, and follow the reading of the sentences in the lesson. There are no substitute words in this section. The teacher asks the students to look at the big picture in the book, and then the teacher reads out the sentence, for example, “她会弹钢琴”. The students point at the picture and repeat the sentence at the same time. The teacher checks students' performance individually.

TEXT TRANSLATION[课文译文]

我会打字。 I can type.

我会游泳。 I can swim.

我会游泳。
Wǒ huì yóuyǒng.
14
I can type
1
97

A Sing and perform 表演唱

歌曲的学习方法参见本书的“使用说明”。

活动方法➡学生们学会歌曲以后，教师组织课堂活动。学生们围成一圈，教师站在中间。教师先做出游泳的动作，学生们一起唱：“谁会游泳？……老师会游泳。……”教师接着做其他的动作，如“打字”、“做饭”等，学生们接着唱歌，直到所有的词语都得到练习。教师也可以找一个学生到圆圈中间表演动作，其他同学唱歌，歌曲中的人名要换成做动作的学生的名字。

歌曲文本➡谁会游泳？谁会游泳？啦啦啦 啦啦啦。老师会游泳。老师会游泳。啦啦啦 啦啦啦。

Refer to the *Teacher Manual* for the method for learning the song in the book.

METHOD ➡ After the students have learned the song, the teacher starts to organize the class activities. The students stand in a circle, the teacher stays in the middle. The teacher first makes a swimming move, then students sing together: “谁会游泳？……老师会游泳。……” Then the teacher moves on to make other gestures, such as “打字”, “做饭”, etc. The students continue to sing songs till all the words get practiced. The teacher can also find a student to come to the middle of the circle to make gestures while the other students sing the song. The person’s name in the song has to be changed to the student’s name, who is making the moves in the middle of the circle.

THE SONG SCRIPT ➡ Who can swim? Who can swim? Lalala lalala. The teacher can swim. The teacher can swim. Lalala lalala.

B Sentence patterns 学句型

Read the patterns aloud, and then find the four children in Page 96-97 and compose sentences with “会”. 大声朗读句型，在96-97页找到下面的四个小朋友，看图用“会”造句。

❶ 这部分是句型总结与复习。教师先领学生反复大声朗读句型框里的句型，直到学生可以流利地读出句型框里的句子。

❶ This section is the summary of the sentence patterns and the reviews. The teacher leads the students in reading out aloud the sentence patterns in the box repeatedly till they can read the sentences fluently.

14

A

Sing and perform 表演唱

Shéi huì yóuyǒng?
Shéi huì yóuyǒng?
Lā lā lā lā lā lā.

Lǎoshī huì yóuyǒng.
Lǎoshī huì yóuyǒng.
Lā lā lā lā lā lā.

98

B

Sentence patterns 学句型

Read the patterns aloud, and then find the four children in Page 96–97 and compose sentences with "会". 大声朗读句型，在96–97页找到下面的四个小朋友，看图用"会"造句。

我 wǒ	会 huì	做饭 zuòfàn
		游泳 yóuyǒng
		画画儿 huàhuàr
我们 wǒmen		弹钢琴 tán gāngqín
		打篮球 dǎ lánqiú

P.96 ______

P.97 ______

P.96 ______

P.97 ______

14 I can type

99

Notes

❷ 学生根据提示，在学生用书第96页和97页找到练习中的四个人物，然后用“他/她会……”造句。可以写汉字，也可以写拼音。教师检查，对全做对的学生给予鼓励或者奖励。

❷ The students find the four people in the exercise on pages 96 and 97 on the Student Book according to the prompts, and then make up sentences with“他/她会……” They can write either in *pinyin* or the characters. The teacher checks their works. The students who have done without any mistakes get encouragement or prizes.

KEY · · 答案

她会弹钢琴。 他会打篮球。 她会做饭。 他会画画儿。

A Interesting characters 趣味汉字

本课学习的汉字是“马”和“书”，要求学生掌握这两个字的正确写法。汉字的教学方法参见本书的“使用说明”。

This lesson teaches the characters “马” and “书”. The students are required to master the correct way of writing these two characters. Refer to the *Teacher Manual* for the teaching method in the book.

B Let's do it 做一做

With two students in a group, one student asks the other what he/she can do, and writes or draws his/her ability. Then introduce your partner's ability to the class. 两个小朋友一组，先问一下你的同伴会做什么事，然后写出或者画出他/她会做的事情，最后向全班同学介绍一下你的同伴。

准备材料 ➡ 铅笔、彩笔

方法 ➡ 两个学生一组，互相问对方会做什么事，然后写出或者画出对方会做的事情。完成以后，每个学生向全班介绍一下同伴会做的事情。

MATERIALS NEEDED ➡ pencils, color pencils

METHOD ➡ Two students are in a group. They introduce to each other about what each can do. Then write out or draw out what the fellow partner can do. After that, each student starts to tell the whole class what his fellow partner can do.

14

A

Interesting characters 趣味汉字

马

horse mǎ

马 马 马 马

书

book shū

书 书 书 书

100

B

Let's do it 做一做

- With two students in a group, one student asks the other what he/she can do, and writes or draws his/her ability. Then introduce your partner's ability to the class.
  两个小朋友一组，先问一下你的同伴会做什么事，然后写出或者画出他/她会做的事情，最后向全班同学介绍一下你的同伴。

我的朋友
my friend

14 I can type

101

Notes

Supplementary activities 补充活动

1. Make small paper box 制作小纸盒

准备材料 剪刀、胶棒、活动页（见附页14.1）

方法 复印足够数量的活动页，发给每个学生一份。学生用剪刀沿实线将图剪下来，然后沿虚线对折，再用胶棒将边缘粘牢，做成一个小纸盒。纸盒做好以后，两个学生一组，轮流扔自己做的纸盒。纸盒落下以后，学生用笔将纸盒朝上的一面做个小标记，并根据这一面上的图案说句子："他/她会……"。每个纸盒有六面，每个学生有10次扔纸盒的机会，在10次内扔到最多相同面数的学生获胜。

MATERIALS NEEDED scissors, glue sticks, Activity Page (See attachment 14.1)

METHOD Make enough copies of the Activity Page. Give each student a copy. The students cut out the pictures along the dotted line with scissors, then fold the pictures along the dotted line, finally, stick the edges together to make a small paper box. After that, two students are in a group, and throws the paper box in turn. After the paper box falls down, the student uses the pencil to make a small mark on the up-facing side, and then makes up a sentence based on the picture on this side: "他/她会……" Each paper box has six sides. Each student has ten chances to throw the paper box. The student with the most number of the same side with ten throws wins in the end.

2. Card game 卡片游戏

准备材料 活动页（见附页14.2）

方法 将活动页复印足够的套数，剪裁成小卡片。学生3～4人一组，每组选一个组长，领取两套卡片。组长将卡片正面朝下摆放在每个小组的桌子上。每组的学生依次说出一项自己会做的事情，如"我会游泳"，说完后翻开一张卡片，如果卡片上的词语和他所说的事情一致，这张卡片就归他所有；如果不一致，就要把卡片放回桌子上，由组长

MATERIALS NEEDED Activity Page (See attachment 14.2)

METHOD Make enough copies of the Activity Page. Cut them out into small cards. Put the students into groups of 3-4. Each group elects a group leader who gets two sets of the cards. The group leader puts the cards face down on their desktop. Students in each group say one thing they can do in turn, for example, "我会游泳". After that he turns over one

重新洗一下牌，下一个学生重新开始说句子。每个学生都有五次说句子、翻卡片的机会。游戏完成后，得到最多卡片的学生获胜。

card. If the card has the same words as he has said, he can keep the card; if not, he has to put back the card on the desktop. Then the group leader reshuffles the cards. The next student starts to say the sentences. Each student has five chances to speak and turn over the cards. At the end of the game, the student with the most cards wins.

3. Whisper 悄悄话

方法▶▶将学生分为两组，每组坐成一排。教师用本课句型想好一个句子，如"××会打字"，同时把这个句子轻声告诉给每组的第一个学生，然后教师说"开始"，第一个学生把听到的句子轻声传给第二个学生，这样依次传下去，最后一个学生把听到的句子写在黑板上（用汉字或拼音均可）。教师在黑板上写出原句，对比一下，写得完全正确的小组获胜。如果时间允许，教师可以多说几个句子，重复这个游戏。

METHOD▶▶Put the students into two groups. Each group sits in a line. The teacher uses the sentence pattern in the lesson to make a sentence, for example, "××会打字". Then he tells the first student in each group the sentence gently. After that, the teacher says: "开始". The first student passes the sentence he has heard to the second student. Follow this way till the last student in each line has heard the sentence, who then writes the sentence (either in *pinyin* or the characters) on the board. The teacher writes out the original sentence on the board for students to compare. The group or groups that make no mistakes win in the end. If time permits, the teacher can say a few more sentences to repeat this game multiple times.

REVIEW 7 复习

A Write, guess and say 写一写，猜一猜，说一说

Write down the names of some activities you can think of. Then ask your partner to guess which of them you know how to do. 写出你能想到的活动名称，让你的同伴猜一猜你会做其中的哪些事。

准备材料 足够数量的长方形纸条或者卡片

方法 两个学生一组，发给每个学生4～6张纸条或者卡片，然后按照学生用书第102页的要求做练习。每个学生在纸条或者卡片上写出至少四个他能想到的活动名称，其中包括自己会做的事情和不会做的事情。每张纸条上只能写一个句子。教师根据学生水平要求学生用拼音或者汉字写句子。写完后，两个学生互相从对方的纸条里猜出对方会做的事情，把纸条拿起来，问对方："你会打字？"（句末用升调）对方回答："是，我会打字"或者"不，我不会打字"。学生在对方会做的事情上做个标记，等双方全部猜完以后，学生分别拿着做了标记的纸条向教师报告："××会……"

对话示例

A：你会……？

B：是，我会……

不，我不会……

MATERIALS NEEDED enough rectangular paper slips or cards

METHOD Two students are in a group. Give each student 4-6 pieces of paper or the cards. Do the practice according to the directions on page 102 in the Student Book. Each student writes down at least four names of the activities that he can think of on the paper slips or the cards, including the things that he both can and can't do. Each paper slip can have only one sentence. The teacher asks the students to write the sentence either in *pinyin* or the characters according to students' learning situation. After that, the two students guess from each other's paper slip what he/she can do. One student picks up a slip and asks the other student:"你会打字？" (Using the rising tone at the end of the sentence.) The answer is either: "是，我会打字" or "不，我不会打字". The student takes notes of the things that his partner can do. After all is done, the two students report to the teacher with the notes: "××会……"

EXAMPLE See the Chinese version on the left.

B Story time 故事会

教学方法参见本书的“使用说明”。

故事文本▶▶明明是个小学生，他很爱吹牛。有一天，他跟美美说：“我会打字。”美美把明明带到电脑前，明明一个字也打不出来。美美明白了，她说：“你不会打字。”丁丁觉得很不好意思，于是他说：“我会游泳。”美美带明明来到游泳池，结果明明喝了好几口水。美美明白了，她说：“你不会游泳。”明明又戴上了一顶厨师的帽子，对美美说：“我会做饭。”美美带明明来到厨房，明明开始炒菜，一不小心，锅里着火了，明明吓了一大跳。美美叹

Refer to the *Teacher Manual* for the teaching method in the book.

STORY TEXT▶▶ Mingming is an elementary student. He likes to brag. One day, he told Meimei: “我会打字。” Meimei then took him to the computer. Mingming couldn't type a word. Meimei realized, and said: “你不会打字。” Mingming felt very embarrassed, and said: “我会游泳。” Meimei took him to a swimming pool. Mingming went down and almost got drowned. Meimei realized, and said: “你不会游泳。” This time Mingming put on a chef's hat and said: “我会做饭。” Meimei brought

了口气，说：“你不会做饭。”那明明到底会做什么呢？

him to the kitchen, and Mingming started to cook a dish. Due to his carelessness, the wok was on fire. Mingming got a big startle. Meimei sighed and said: “你不会做饭。” What on earth can Mingming do?

TRANSLATION[译文] 图1：我会打字。I can type.

图2：你不会打字。You can not type.

图3：我会游泳。I can swim.

图4：你不会游泳。You can not swim.

图5：我会做饭。I can cook.

图6：你不会做饭。You can not cook.

Unit Eight 第八单元

第十五课：城市
第十六课：我想去中国

教学目标：❶ 复习声母和韵母
Objectives ❷ 句型：……想去……

生词：中国 · 北京 · 上海 · 昆明 · 香港 · 放假 · 了 · 想 · 去
New Words

语言点：“想”的用法
Language Point

日常用语：自我介绍
Daily ExpresSions

汉字：雨 网
Chinese Characters

活动：制作城市招贴画
Activity

Introduction 导入

❶ 教师事先让学生准备一些自己喜爱的明星的照片，并调查这些明星会做哪些事情。上课时，教师让学生分别展示自己准备的明星照片，同时问学生："他是谁？他会做什么？"学生用汉语或英语回答。以此复习前一个单元学习的内容。对于本书没有学过的词语，学生可以用母语表达，教师将其翻译成中文，并写在黑板上，作为补充词语教给学生。

❷ 教师准备一张世界地图（或者一个地球仪）、两张中国地图。上课时，教师用中文或英文问学生："你知道哪些地方？你想去哪些地方？"学生在世界地图或者地球仪上指出自己想去的国家或者城市，随后教师指着地图上的中国，说："今天我们学习中国和中国的城市。"教师利用本课的词语卡片，先教学生学会"中国"，以及"北京"、"上海"、"昆明"、"香港"四个城市的名称，随后将学生分为两组，做两个小游戏：（1）发给每组一张中国地图，学生在地图上找出本课学习的四个城市，并贴上一个小标记，在最短时间内全部找到的一组获胜；（2）教师把中国地图贴在黑板上，每组派一个学生到黑板前，教师任意说一个城市名，两个学生快速指出相应的地点，先指对的学生所在的小组加1分。重复这个游戏，直到所有的学生都得到练习。得分最多的小组获胜。

❶ The teacher asks the students to prepare some photos of their favorite stars, and investigate the things these stars can do. In class, the teacher has the students display these photos, and asks at the same time: "他是谁？他会做什么？" The students answer in Chinese. For the words which have not been taught in Unit Seven, students can express in English, the teacher then translates them into Chinese and writes them on the board as the supplementary words in order to review the contents of the previous unit.

❷ The teacher prepares a world map (or a globe), and two China maps. In class, the teacher asks the students either in Chinese or English: "你知道哪些地方？你想去哪些地方？(Which places do you know? Where do you want to go?)" The students point at the cities or countries where they want to go on the world map or on the globe. Then the teacher points at China on the map and says: "今天我们学习中国和中国的城市。(Today we are going to study China and the Chinese cities.)" The teacher uses the word cards in the lesson to teach the students to learn "中国", "北京", "上海", "昆明", and "香港". Then he puts the students into two groups to do two mini games: (1) give each group a China map. Have the students find and mark the four cities to be learned in the lesson on the map. The group that does the job in the shortest possible time wins; (2) the teacher sticks the China map on the board. Each group sends a student to the board. The teacher says a city name at random, the two students point at the corresponding place on the map as quickly as possible. The student who gets it right wins a point for his group. Repeat the game till all the students get a chance to practice. The group with the highest point wins in the end.

第15课 城市
chéng shì

Let's read 读一读

b p m f d t n l g k h

j q x z c s zh ch sh r y w

a o e i u ü

104

Notes

Cities 城市 15

Let's read 读一读

复习学过的声母和韵母。

Review the pronunciations of the initials and finals learned in this book.

A Exercise 练一练

Listen and choose the *pinyin* you hear. 听录音，在听到的拼音前面画√。

KEY · · 答案

1. línshí	2. jīguāng	3. chīlí
4. sànxīn	5. dúshū	6. cháimén
7. zhìdù	8. xiǎochī	9. zuìchún
10. xièxie	11. báiyún	12. yuǎnshì

B Let's recognize 认一认

这部分是本课学习的词语，教学方法参见本书的“使用说明”。

This section teaches the words in the lesson. Refer to the *Teacher Manual* for the teaching method.

SUPPLEMENTARY WORDS [补充生词]

大连 Dalian Dàlián | 洛阳 Luoyang Luòyáng | 郑州 Zhengzhou Zhèngzhōu | 西安 Xi'an Xī'ān |

南京 Nanjing Nánjīng | 成都 Chengdu Chéngdū | 重庆 Chongqing Chóngqìng | 拉萨 Lasa Lāsà |

乌鲁木齐 Ulumuqi Wūlǔmùqí

A

Chinese

Exercise 练一练

• Listen and choose the *pinyin* you hear. 听录音，在听到的拼音前画√。

①	• línshí	• língshí	②	• jīguān	• jīguāng
③	• chīlì	• chīlí	④	• sànxīn	• shànxīn
⑤	• dúshū	• túshū	⑥	• zháimén	• cháimén
⑦	• zhìdù	• jìdù	⑧	• xiǎoqì	• xiǎochī
⑨	• zuìchún	• zuǐchún	⑩	• jiějie	• xièxie
⑪	• báiyún	• báiyín	⑫	• yǎnshì	• yuǎnshì

15 Cities

105

15

Let's recognize 认一认

B

中国
Zhōngguó

北京
Běijīng

上海
Shànghǎi

昆明
Kūnmíng

香港
Xiānggǎng

放假	fàngjià	to be on holiday			
了	le	(an auxiliary particle)			
想	xiǎng	want	去	qù	go

106

Notes

Exercises 练一练

1. Listen and choose the right words. 听录音，在正确的答案前面画√。

KEY··答案

1. Shànghǎi　　2. Běijīng
3. Kūnmíng　　4. Xiānggǎng

2. Listen and match. 听录音，连线。

KEY··答案

录音文本：
1. 昆明
2. 北京
3. 上海
4. 香港

Activity 课堂活动

Draw or paste photos related with your daily life, and then introduce yourself to your class. Please use the sentence patterns below. 在相框中画出或者贴上与你日常生活相关的照片，然后向全班介绍一下自己吧！请使用下面的句型。

准备材料 学生自己的生活照、彩笔、胶棒

方法 教师按照学生用书第108页的要求指导学生做练习。学生在相框中画出或者贴上与自己日常生活相关的图片或

MATERIALS NEEDED the life photos of the students', color pencils, glue sticks

METHOD Do the exercise on page 108 in the Student Book. The students draw or stick their daily life pictures or photos in the picture frames. Then they learn to introduce themselves after the sentence patterns under the frames. After they

A

Exercise 练一练

1 Listen and choose the right words. 听录音，在正确的答案前画√。

①

- Shànghǎi
- Shānghǎi
- Shànghǎn

②

- Běijīng
- Běiqīng
- Běixīng

③

- Kūnníng
- Kūnmíng
- Kūnlíng

④

- Xiānggǎng
- Xiāngǎng
- Xīnggǎng

15 Cities

2 Listen and match. 听录音，连线。

kūn  hǎi

běi  jīng

shàng  míng

xiāng  gǎng

107

15

B

Activity 课堂活动

- Draw or paste photos related with your daily life, and then introduce yourself to your class. Please use the sentence patterns below. 在相框中画出或者贴上与你日常生活相关的照片，然后向全班介绍一下自己吧！请使用下面的句型。

我叫____。我____岁。我是____国人。我住在____。
我读____年级。我学习____。我家有____。

Wǒ jiào ____. wǒ ____ suì. wǒ shì ____ guórén. wǒ zhù zài ____.
wǒ dú ____ niánjí. wǒ xuéxí ____. wǒ jiā yǒu ____.

108

Notes

者照片，然后按照相框下边所给的句型提示，练习自我介绍。学生完成相框设计以后，分别拿着课本到教室前边，一边展示图片一边介绍自己。教师在旁边指导并给予鼓励。如果学生的汉语水平较低，教师可以先领学生学习本单元的“说一说”，等学生熟悉掌握了自我介绍的常用句子以后，再完成这个课堂活动。

are done with the design of frames, they come to the front with their textbooks respectively, showing their photos and introducing themselves. The teacher gives directions and encouragement on the side. If their Chinese level is low the teacher can first guide them finishing the *Let's say* section in this unit. After the students get familiar with the frequently used sentences for self introduction, they can then complete this class activity.

Let's say 说一说

教学方法参见本书的“使用说明”。

Refer to the *Teacher Manual* for the teaching method in the book.

Let's say 说一说

A

我叫杰克。我十岁。我是美国人。
Wǒ jiào Jiékè. Wǒ shí suì. Wǒ shì Měiguórén.

我住在纽约。我读四年级。我学习汉语。
Wǒ zhù zài Niǔyuē. Wǒ dú sì niánjí. Wǒ xuéxí hànyǔ.

我家有四口人，爸爸，妈妈，姐姐和我。
Wǒ jiā yǒu sì kǒu rén, bàba, māma, jiějie hé wǒ.

My name is Jack. I am ten. I am an American. I live in New York. I am in the fourth grade. I study Chinese. There are four people in my family, dad, mom, elder sister and I.

Supplementary activities 补充活动

1. Listen to the teacher and fill in the chart 听音填表

准备材料▶活动页（见附页15.1）

方法▶复印活动页中的拼音表格，发给每个学生一份。教师读出若干音节，每个音节先读声母，再读韵母，最后读声韵拼合，如：b—ā—bā，每组可以读3～5遍，以便给学生充足的时间在表格里找到相应的声母和韵母。学生找到正确的位置后，在该位置上写出音节，如“bā”，也可以只写出声调。学生完成以后，教师把表格收上来检查，给出成绩或者评价。

活动扩展▶教师可以根据附录中的《普通话声韵拼合表》，针对学生在学习过程中容易出现错误的拼音自制表格，进行强化练习。

参考音节▶请参见本书附录中的《普通话声韵拼合表》

MATERIALS NEEDED▶Activity Page (See attachment 15.1)

METHOD▶Make copies of the *pinyin* Chart on the Activity Page. Give each student a copy. The teacher reads out many syllables. Read initial letter first and then the final letter, finally, the combination of the initial and final letters, for example, b—ā—bā. Read each group for 3-5 times so that the students have enough time to find the initial and final letters. The students find the corresponding position and write out the syllables at the location. The students can write out the tonal marks only. After they have completed the task, the teacher collects the charts for check, and gives grades or evaluations.

EXPANDED ACTIVITY▶The teacher can self make the *pinyin* chart targeted at the frequently mistaken sounds by the students based on the *Chart for Mandarin Initial and Final Combinations* in the Attachment to reinforce the exercise.

SYLLABLES FOR REFERENCE▶Refer to the *Chart for Mandarin Initial and Final Combinations* in the attachment in the book.

2. Word matching game 组词游戏

准备材料▶剪刀、胶棒、活动页（见附页15.2）

方法▶学生两人一组，复印活动页，发给每组一份。学生先把活动页上的汉字剪下来，然后将汉字拼成正确的城市

MATERIALS NEEDED▶scissors, glue sticks, Activity Page (See attachment 15.2)

METHOD▶Two students are in a group. Make copies of the Activity Page. Give each group a copy. The students cut out the characters from

名称，并粘贴在相应的城市图片旁边。学生完成以后，举手示意，教师走到学生身边，检查结果，同时给予鼓励或者奖励。

the Activity Page first, and then put the characters into the correct city names, and finally, stick them to the corresponding pictures of the cities. After that, they raise their hands to draw the teacher's attention. The teacher comes to the student and checks his works, giving encouragement or the prize at the same time.

3. Guess who is he/she 猜猜他/她是谁

准备材料 ➽ 若干张白纸卡、一个空盒子

方法 ➽ 发给每个学生一张白纸卡。学生在白纸卡的右下角写上自己的名字，然后在纸上用拼音或者汉字写出关于自己的情况，如年龄、生日、家庭成员、自己的爱好、会做的事情、所在的城市等。写完后，学生根据纸卡上的内容向全班介绍自己，随后把纸卡放在空盒子里。全班学生的纸卡都放到盒子里以后，教师可以组织课堂活动：找学生从盒子里抽一张纸卡，把上边的内容读出来，其他学生根据内容猜一猜这是谁写的纸卡。重复这个游戏，直到所有的学生都得到练习。

MATERIALS NEEDED ➽ some white paper cards, an empty box

METHOD ➽ Give each student a piece of white paper. The students write down their names on the bottom right of the white paper card, and then write about their personal information in either Chinese or English on the paper, such as age, birthday, family members, hobbies, the things they can do, the city. After that, the students start to introduce themselves to the class based on the information on the card, and then put the cards in the empty box. After all students have placed their cards in the box, the teacher can organize the class activity: ask a student to pull out a card from the box, and then read it out. The other students try to guess who wrote the card based on the information. Continue the game till all the students have a chance to practice.

16 I want to go to China 我想去中国

A Let's learn 学一学

❶ 本课学习表示意愿的动词"想"，句型的基本格式是"主语+想+宾语"，其中宾语通常是动词短语，例如"我想去北京"，"我想吃苹果"。"想"的否定形式是"不想"，例如"我不想吃苹果"。

❷ 另外，本课首次出现助词"了"，即"放假了"。"了"的用法比较复杂，我们在第3～6册中会陆续学习"了"的几种主要用法。在本课，"了"说明在特定时间内某个动作已经发生或者某种情况已经出现，即表示在说话的时候"放假"这个情况已经出现了。在这里，教师不必从语法角度讲解"了"，只是把"放假了"作为一个固定格式教给学生，以降低汉语学习的难度，以避免使学生产生畏难情绪。

❸ 教师利用本单元的词语卡片组织课堂活动：（1）教师把词语卡片贴在黑板上，先领读词语，然后做示范：教师说："老师想去北京"，说完后一下子跳到卡片"北京"的下边，然后接着说："老师想去上海"，说完后跳到卡片"上海"的下边，以此类推，直到所有的词语都得到练习。教师示范后，找学生按照这个方法来做游戏，即教师说句子："××想去……"，学生跳到相应的卡片下边。（2）四个学生一组，

❶ This lesson teaches the verb "想" expressing desire. Its basic structure goes like this: subject + "想" + object. The verbal phrase always functions as object. For example, "我想去北京", "我想吃苹果". The negative form of "想" is "不想". For example, "我不想吃苹果".

❷ In addition, the particle "了" appears for the first time in this lesson, i.e., "放假了". The usage of "了" is fairly complicated. We'll learn a few of the primary usage of "了" in volume 3 through volume 6 step by step. In this lesson, "了" expresses the idea that something has already happened, i.e., "放假了" has already happened at the time of speaking. In the class, the teacher need not explain "了" from the grammar point. Just teach "放假了" as a set phrase to lower the difficulty level in learning Chinese and avoid the students' fear of and reluctance for Chinese.

❸ The teacher uses the word cards in the lesson to organize the class activity: (1) the teacher sticks the word cards on the board, and then leads in reading the words, finally does the demonstration: the teacher says: "老师想去北京". After that, he jumps under the card "北京", then he goes on to say: "老师想去上海". After that he jumps under

第16课 我想去中国

wǒ xiǎng qù zhōng guó

Let's learn 学一学

离黑板远一些，站到一条线上。教师说“开始”，学生快速跑到黑板前抢一张卡片，然后站成一排，根据抢来的卡片说句子：“我想去……”

❹ 活动做完后，学生回到座位，打开书，看图，听录音，跟读课本中的句子。这部分配有替换词语，可以用来进行替换练习。练习前教师把句型“我/他想去……”写在黑板上，然后教师指着替换部分的第一幅图做示范：模仿男学生的声音说“我想去上海”，或者用自己的声音说“他想去上海”，学生跟读。示范后，教师任意指一幅图，找学生说出句子。学生说完后，教师说一遍正确的句子，全班学生跟读。

the card “上海”. Continue the game till all the words get practiced. After the demonstration, the teacher asks the students to start the game by this way. The teacher says sentence: “××想去……” the students then jump under the corresponding card. (2) Four students are in a group. Stay away from the board, stand in one line. The teacher says “开始”, the students run to the board to grab a card and then stand in a line, speak the sentence according to the card grabbed: “我想去……”

❹ After the game, the students return to their seats, open the books, look at the picture, listen to the recording, and follow reading the sentences in the lesson. This section is provided the substitute words, which can be used for the substitution drill. Before the drill, the teacher puts the sentence pattern “我/他想去……” on the board, and then the teacher points at the first picture in the substitute section to do a demonstration, imitating a boy student's voice: “我想去上海”, or uses his own voice: “他想去上海”. After the demonstration, the teacher points at any picture and asks a few students to try to say the sentences. After the students have tried, the teacher says the correct sentence once, the whole class follows him.

TEXT TRANSLATION[课文译文]

放假了。 It is time for vacation.

我想去中国。 I want to go to China.

B PATTERN'S SUBSTITUTE[句型替换]

我/他想去上海。 我/她想去北京。

我/他想去昆明。 我/她想去香港。

Let's try 试一试

______ 想 去 ______ 。
xiǎng qù

16 I want to go to China

A Pass the ball and sing 传皮球，唱一唱

歌曲的学习方法请参见本书的“使用说明”。

准备材料 ➡ 小皮球

活动方法 ➡ 学生们学会歌曲以后，教师组织课堂活动。学生分为两组，面对面，各站成一排。A组的一个学生拿着小皮球，任选一个自己想去的城市，然后唱出来：“北京，北京，去北京。我想去北京。”一边唱一边把皮球任意扔给B组的一个学生，B组学生接到皮球以后，接着唱下去“北京，北京，去北京，他想去北京。”也可以把“他”换成A组扔球学生的名字。如果B组学生唱对了，就可以选一个自己想去的城市名称，接着唱下去，然后把球扔给A组的一个学生；如果唱错了，就要站到A组里来，A组重新选一个学生开始这个游戏。游戏结束后，教师数一数两组学生的人数，人数多的一组获胜。

歌曲文本 ➡ 北京，北京，去北京。我想去北京。上海，上海，去上海。我想去上海。

Refer to the *Teacher Manual* for the method for learning the song in the book.

MATERIALS NEEDED ➡ a small leather ball

METHOD ➡ After the students have learned the song, the teacher starts to organize the class activity: put the students into two groups. Stand in line, face to face. The student from Group A holds a small leather ball. He chooses a city he wants to go to and then sings out: “北京，北京，去北京。我想去北京。” He sings and throws the ball to a student in Group B, who after catching the ball and continues to sing “北京，北京，去北京。他想去北京。” He can also change “他” into Group A’s student’s name who threw the ball. If the student from Group B sang it correctly, he could choose the name of the city he wants to go, and continues to sing, and then throws the ball to a student from Group A. If he sang incorrectly, he would stand among the students in Group A , which sends another student to start the game. After the game, the teacher counts the number of the students from the two groups. The group with more students wins in the end.

THE SONG SCRIPT ➡ Beijing, Beijing, go to Beijing. I want to go to Beijing. Shanghai, Shanghai, go to Shanghai. I want to go to Shanghai.

B Sentence patterns 学句型

Write the names of the cities. Read aloud the patterns, and then answer the questions with “想” according to the colors of the stars. 写出城市名称。大声朗读句型，然后根据星星的颜色用“想”回答问题。

16 A

Pass the ball and sing 传皮球，唱一唱

Běijīng, Běijīng, qù Běijīng.
Wǒ xiǎng qù Běijīng.

Běijīng, Běijīng, qù Běijīng.
Tā xiǎng qù Běijīng.

Shànghǎi, Shànghǎi, qù Shànghǎi.
Wǒ xiǎng qù Shànghǎi.

Shànghǎi, Shànghǎi, qù Shànghǎi.
Tā xiǎng qù Shànghǎi.

112

B

Sentence patterns 学句型

- Write the names of the cities. Read aloud the patterns, and then answer the questions with "想" according to the colors of the stars. 写出城市名称。大声朗读句型，然后根据星星的颜色用"想"回答问题。

B ____

Sh ____

X ____

K ____

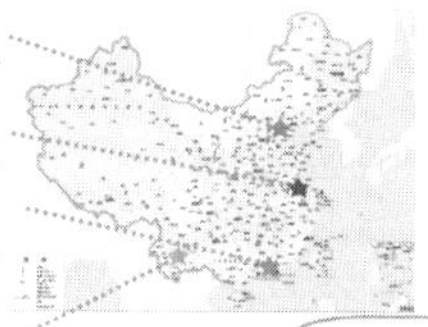

我 wǒ	想 xiǎng	去 qù	中国 Zhōngguó
我们 wǒmen			北京 Běijīng

Which city do the children want to go to?

I want to go to China

16

113

Notes

❶ 这部分是句型总结与复习。学生先自己完成第一部分的内容，根据地图写出拼音，要特别注意地图中代表每个城市的星星的颜色。

❷ 教师先领学生反复大声朗读句型框里的句型，直到学生可以流利地读出句型框里的句子。学生根据第1题和本题中星星的颜色用“我/他想去……”造句，可以用拼音或者汉字写出答案，教师个别指导 。

❶ This section is the summary of the sentence patterns and the reviews. The students complete the first section first, write out the *pinyin* according to the map. Special attention should be given to the colors of the stars representing each city on the map.

❷ The teacher first leads the students in reading out loud the sentence patterns in the box repeatedly till they can read them fluently. Students look at the picture, answer the questions using “我/他想去……” based on the colors of the stars, or write out the answers in *pinyin* or the characters. The teacher supervises individually.

KEY · · 答案

他想去北京。 她想去上海。 他想去昆明。 她想去香港。

A Interesting characters 趣味汉字

本课学习的汉字是“雨”和“网”，要求学生掌握这两个字的正确写法。汉字的教学方法参见本书的“使用说明”。

This lesson teaches the characters “雨” and “网”. The Students are required to master the correct way of writing these two characters. Refer to the *Teacher Manual* for the teaching method in the book.

B Let's do it 做一做

Make a poster: Our city 做招贴画：我们的城市

准备材料 ▶▶ 胶棒、大白纸、城市的照片或图片、彩笔

方法 ▶▶ 学生提前准备自己所在城市的照片或图片，最好是有代表性的建筑、景观、人物、动物、食物等等，用剪刀仔细地把图剪下来，然后用胶棒粘贴在大白纸上，然后在四周画一些装饰性的

MATERIALS NEEDED ▶▶ glue sticks, a piece of large white paper, the photos or the pictures of the city, color pens

METHOD ▶▶ Students prepare the photos and the pictures of the city they live in beforehand. The best pictures are those signature build-

16

Interesting characters 趣味汉字

A

雨

rain yǔ

雨 雨 雨 雨

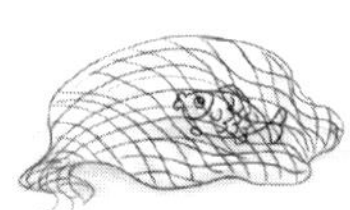

网

net wǎng

网 网 网 网

114

Let's do it 做一做

B

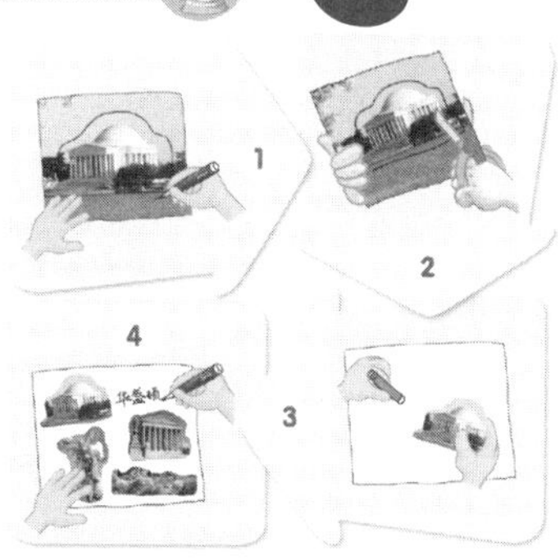

- Make a poster: Our city 做招贴画：我们的城市

16 I want to go to China

115

Notes

图案，最后写出城市的名称和自己的名字。做完后，教师可以组织一个全班的作品展览。

ings, scenery, people, animals, foods etc. Cut them out with a scissors, and then stick them on the large white paper, finally draw some decorative designs, and write out the city's name and the student's name. The teacher can organize an exhibition for the whole class's works.

Supplementary activities 补充活动

1. Great Wall puzzle 长城拼图

准备材料 剪刀、胶棒、活动页（见附页16.1）

方法 复印足够数量的活动页，发给每个学生一份。学生先将大图涂上颜色，然后沿着虚线将图片剪成小块，参照活动页上方的长城小图，将小块拼合成一张完整的长城图。

MATERIALS NEEDED scissors, glue sticks, Activity Page (See attachment 16.1)

METHOD Make enough copies of the Activity Page. Give each student a copy. Students first paint the big picture with colors, and then cut it up into small pieces along the dotted line. Reference the miniature picture of the Great Wall on top of the Activity Page; piece together the small puzzles into a complete picture of the Great Wall.

2. Throw dice 掷色子

准备材料 若干个色子、若干个棋子、活动页（见附页16.2）

方法 学生2～3人一组，将活动页放大复印后，发给每组一份，同时发给每个学生一个棋子，每组一个色子。学生依次用色子掷出数字，然后根据数字走棋子。例如，数字是3就走3步，以此类推。当棋子停到某个小格里时，如果小格里没有要求，棋子不动，等待下一轮掷色子；如果小格里有要求，学生则要根据要求做出相应的回答，回答正确可

MATERIALS NEEDED a number of dices, and chess pieces, Activity Page (See attachment 16.2)

METHOD Put students into groups of 2-3. Make enlarged copies of the Activity Page and then give each group a copy, a dice and a chess piece to each student at the same time. Students throw dice in turn, and then move their chess pieces according to the number on the dice. For example, number three on the dice means three steps to move. Play

以继续参加游戏，回答错误则要停走一次。每组成员按顺序掷色子，直到所有学生到达终点。最先到达终点的学生获胜。

the game this way. When the chess piece is in a square where there is no demand, it stays there till the next round of dice throwing; otherwise, the student responds accordingly. If he can answer the question correctly, he can continue with the game. If not, he has to stop throwing the dice once. The group members throw the dice in turn till all the students reach the destination. The student who reaches the destination first wins in the end.

3. Beat the drum and pass the flower 击鼓传花

准备材料 ➡ 小鼓和鼓锤（或者盘子和筷子）、绢花

方法 ➡ 全班学生围坐成圈，教师坐在中间负责敲鼓（或者盘子）。教师闭上眼睛，说“开始”，然后开始敲鼓，学生们则开始传绢花。教师随时可以停止敲鼓，鼓声停止的时候绢花在谁的手上谁就要用教师说的一个词语造句。教师可以事先准备好词语卡片，也可以当场口头说出词语。

参考词语 ➡ 想、去、中国、北京、上海、昆明、香港

MATERIALS NEEDED ➡ a small drum and hammer (or a plate and chopsticks), silk flower

METHOD ➡ Students sit in a circle. The teacher sits in the middle beating the drum (or plate). The teacher closes his eyes, and says “开始”, and then starts to beat the drum. The student starts to pass the flower. The teacher can stop beating the drum anytime. When he stops, whoever has the flower should make up a sentence with the word the teacher given. The teacher can prepare the word cards beforehand or improvises.

REFERENCE WORDS ➡ See the Chinese version on the left.

REVIEW 8 复习

A little investigation 小调查

Look at the pictures and ask your partners which city they want to go to. Color one star for each that is chosen. Let's see which city is the most popular. 看下边的图片，问一问你的同伴们想去哪个城市。每当有人选中一个城市，就在相应的图片下面涂上一个小星星。看看哪个城市最受欢迎。

方法➤按照学生用书第116页的要求做调查。每个学生随意去采访10个同学，分别问同学们想去哪个城市。每当有人选中一个城市，采访者就在相应的城市图片下涂一个小星星。采访结束后，每个学生做一个城市排名，然后向全班汇报一下，哪些城市最受欢迎。

活动扩展➤教师可以将这个部分布置为一个家庭作业，让学生回家调查家人想去哪个城市，上课时汇报调查结果。另外，教师也可以在调查中加入更多的城市。

对话示例➤A：你想去哪里？

B：我想去……。

METHOD➤Start the investigation after the directions on page 116 in the Student Book. Each student interviews ten students at random, asking respectively which city these fellow classmates want to go. Every time someone selects a city the interviewer marks it with a little star on the corresponding picture of that city. After the interview each student makes a list of the cities, and then reports to the whole class which cities are the most popular ones among the students in the class.

EXPANDED ACTIVITY➤The teacher may assign this section as the homework requiring students to interview their family members which city they want to visit. When in class, they report their investigative findings. Moreover, the teacher can add more cities in their investigation.

EXAMPLE➤See the Chinese version on the left.

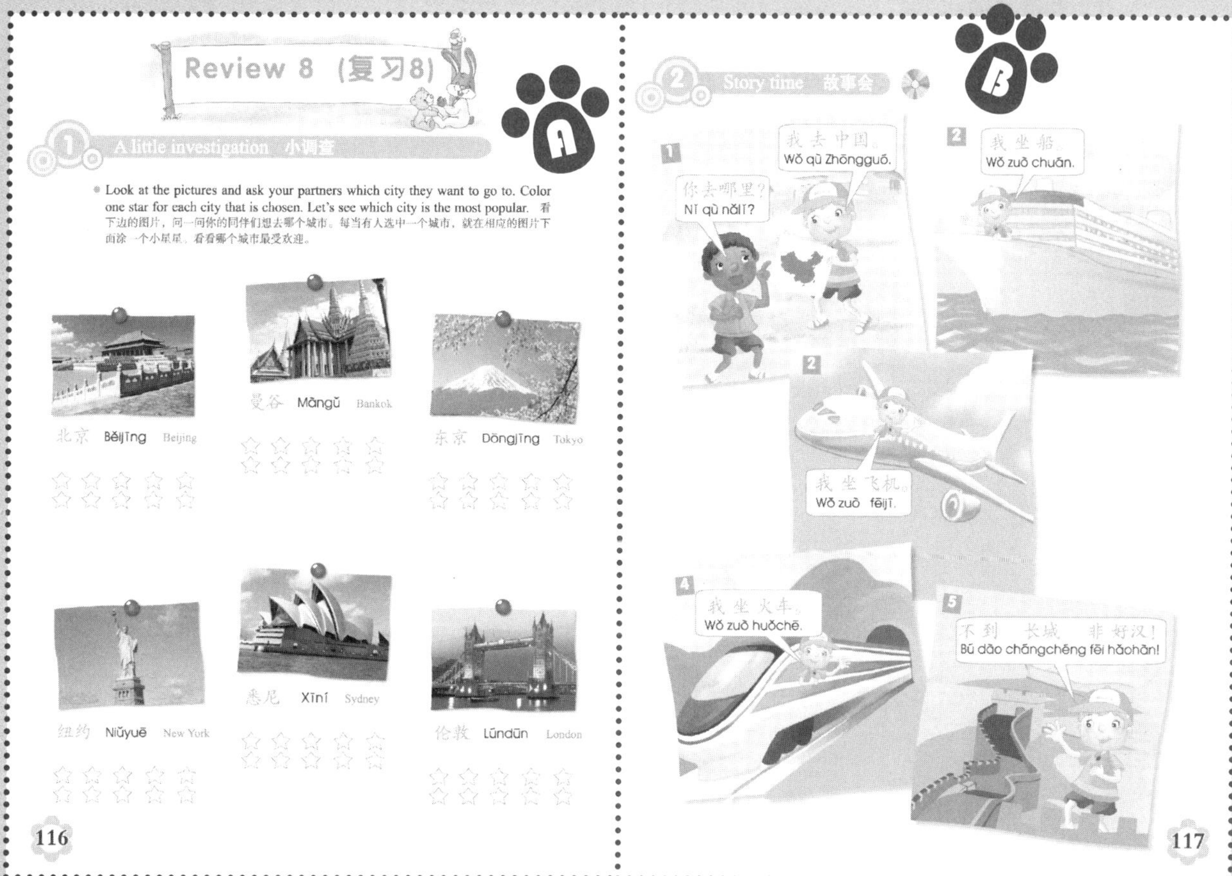

Story time 故事会

教学方法参见本书的“使用说明”。

故事文本▶▶放假了，杰克打算去旅行。汤姆问杰克：“你去哪里？”杰克说：“我去中国。”中国很远很远，杰克先坐船，他说：“我坐船。”然后杰克坐飞机，他说“我坐飞机。”然后杰克坐火车，他说：“我坐火车。”杰克终于到了中国。他登上了长城，高兴地说：“不到长城非好汉！”

Refer to the *Teacher Manual* for the teaching method in the book.

STORY TEXT▶▶It's vacation time. Jack plans to travel. Tom asks Jack: “你去哪里？” Jack says: “我去中国。” Since China is very far away, Jack plans to go by boat. He says: “我坐船。” Then Jack takes the airplane. He says: “我坐飞机。” Then Jack gets on the train. He says: “我坐火车。” Jack arrived in China finally. He climbed on the Great Wall and said proudly: “不到长城非好汉！”

TRANSLATION[译文] ➡ 图1：你去哪里？Where are you going?

我去中国。I am going to China.

图2：我坐船。I am on the boat.

图3：我坐飞机。I am on the airplane.

图4：我坐火车。I am on the train.

图5：不到长城非好汉！You are not a true hero unless you have climbed on the Great Wall.

1.1 Look for the balloons 找气球

Listen to the teacher and paint the *pinyin* in the balloons with your favorite colors. After that, read out your answers.

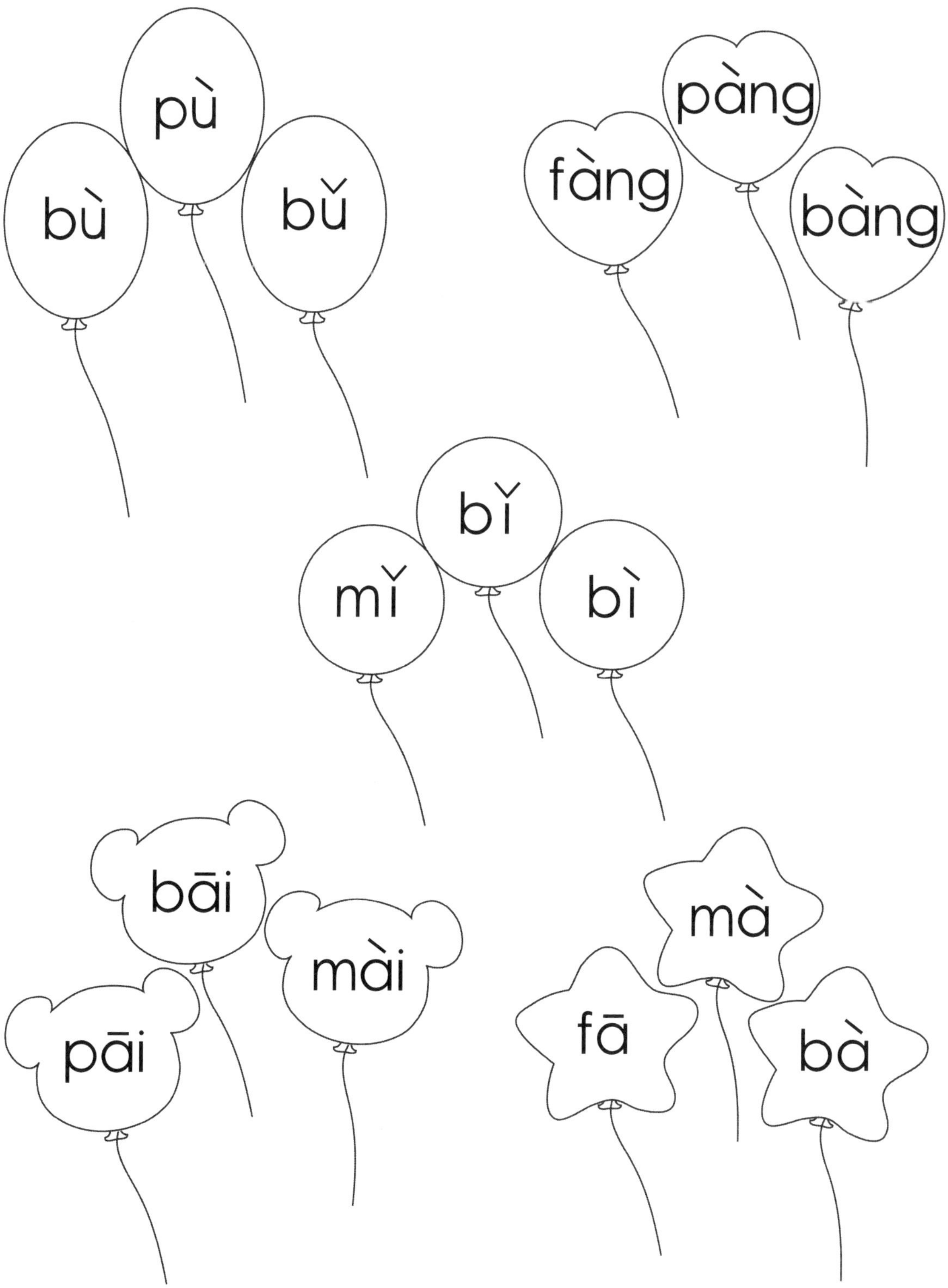

1.2 Listening while writing 边听边写

Two students are in a group. Listen to your teacher and write down the serial number at the corresponding position by turns. Compete to see which group can finish the task fast and well.

2.1 Arrange sentences with the characters 汉字拼句

Cut out the Chinese characters and the punctuations in the form, and then arrange the characters into the four sentences given. After done, raise your hand to get the teacher's attention and read out the sentences.

（1）大象的鼻子很长。（2）爸爸的手很大。
（3）熊猫的尾巴很短。（4）我的手很小。

我	手	手	猫	短
小	熊	象	手	大
的	的	的	的	爸
很	很	很	很	子
手	大	爸	长	鼻
。	。	。	。	

2.2 Look for the Same picture 找相同

Two students are in a group. One holds Picture A and the other holds Picture B. You can't look at each other's picture. There is only one drawing in each picture that is identical, and the rest of the drawings all have different places. Please find the identical drawings from the two pictures through dialogue.

对话示例：XX的……很……

A：美美的裙子很长。

B：美美的裙子很短。

2.3 Look and paste 找一找，粘一粘

Cut out the objects from the left picture. Listen to your teacher and paste the corresponding objects onto the right picture. Then try to describe your picture in Chinese.

3.2 Look for friends 找朋友

Match the characters to make words according to the cue, and then write down the *pinyin* of the words. Compete to see who finishes the task fast and well within the time given.

可	明	→		smart
聪	师	→		teacher
学	生	→		student
他	爱	→		cute
漂	发	→		hair
头	亮	→		pretty
老	们	→		they

3.3 Grab the cards 抢卡片

Listen to your teacher and grab the corresponding character card as quickly as you can. Hold it up upon finding it. Compete to see which student grabs the most cards in the end.

好	棒	真	它
帅	们	口	田

他们	可爱
聪明	漂亮

4.1 Arrange sentences with the characters 汉字拼句

Cut out the Chinese characters and the punctuations in the form, and then arrange the characters into the four sentences given. After done, the student raises his hand to get the teacher's attention and read out the sentences.

（1）你的哥哥真帅！　　（2）妈妈真漂亮！
（3）猴子真聪明！　　（4）她们真棒！

的	子	漂	明
真	妈	猴	你
亮	真	真	她
聪	帅	妈	真
们	哥	哥	棒
！	！	！	！

4.2 Cut, paste and paint 剪一剪，粘一粘，涂一涂

Cut out the small pictures in the picture A and store them for future use. Listen to your teacher and choose the correct small pictures according to the teacher's sentences, and then paste them onto the corresponding people or animals in the picture B. Finally, paint the picture B with the color pens.

A

B

5.1 Look for stars 找星星

Listen to your teacher and paint the stars which has the sound with your favorite colors. Then read out your answers.

hǔ gǔ kǔ

gè hè kè

guā guà guǎ

hěn hèn hèng

kūn kuài kùn

5.2 Arrange and write out the *pinyin* 排一排，写拼音

Please spell out the correct *Pinyin* based on the characters provided, and write them out next to the characters. Compete to see who can finish the task fast and well.

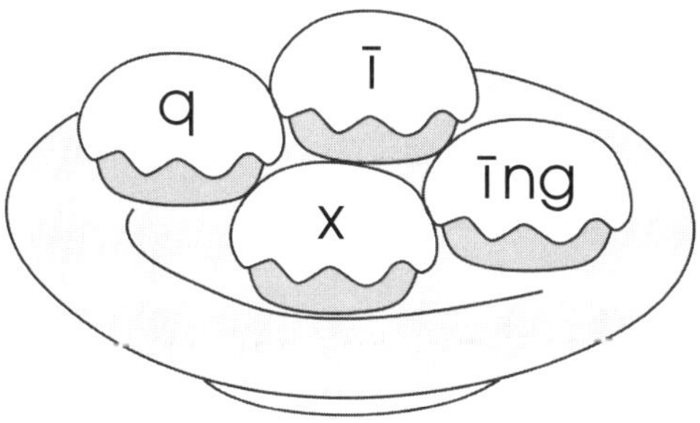

星期

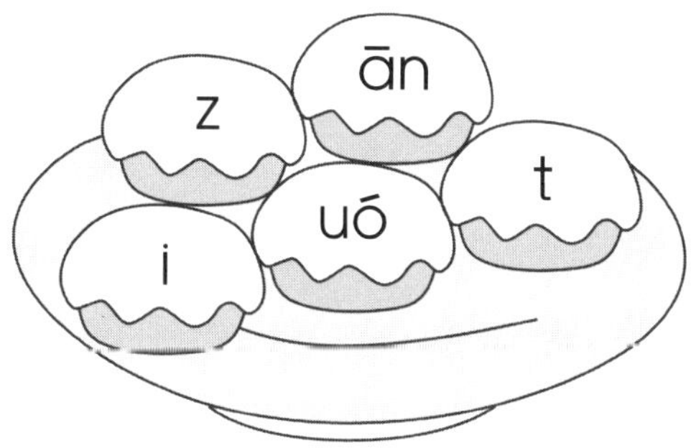

昨天

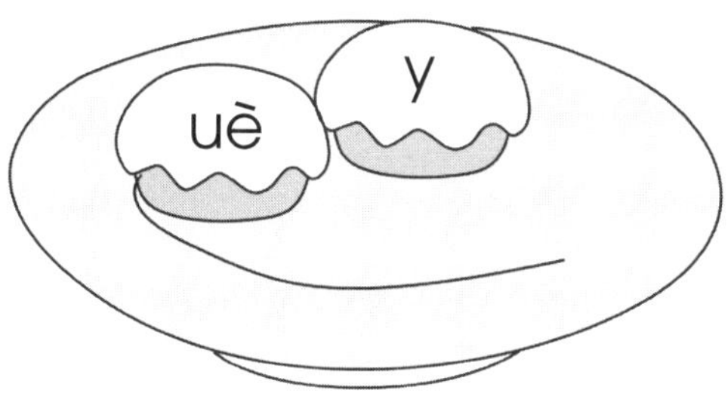

月

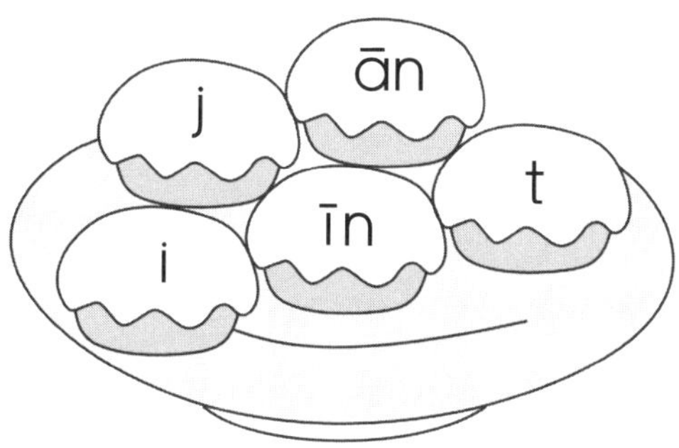

今天

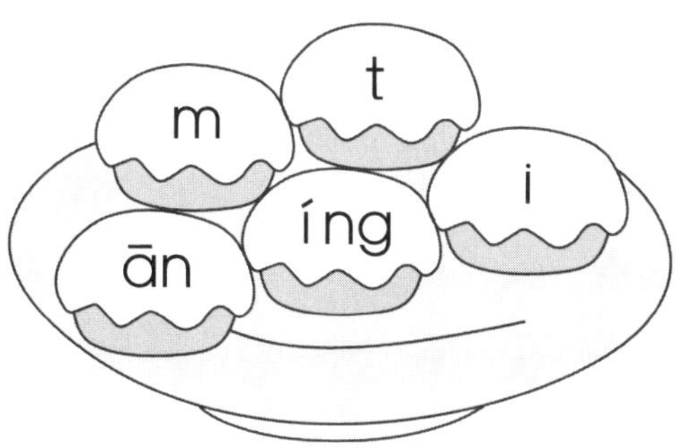

明天

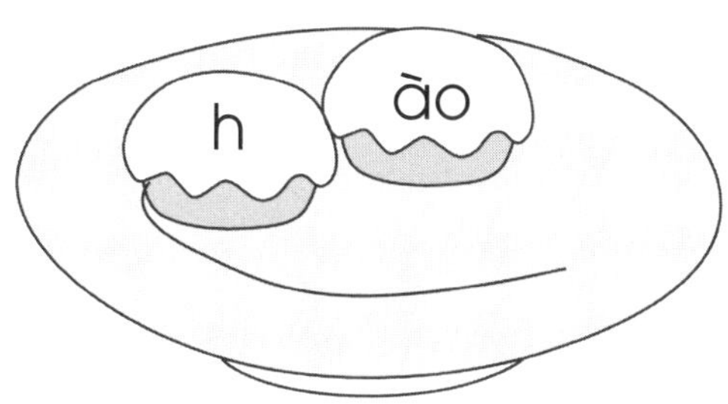

号

6.1 Match the sentences 句子配对

Two students are in a group. First cut out the sentences, and then find the sentences with the same meaning. After done, raises your hand to get the teacher's attention. One student reads out the English sentence, the other reads out the corresponding Chinese sentence. Compete to see which group can finish the task fast and best.

今天十月五号。
明天星期天。
昨天十月五号。
今天星期六。
Today is Saturday.
Tomorrow is Sunday.
Today is October 5.
Yesterday was October 5.

6.3 Think and write down the dates 想一想，写日期

First fill out the dates and then play games with your teacher.

2010年6月

星期日	星期一	星期二	星期三	星期四	星期五	星期六
			16			

7.1 Help out 帮帮忙

In the store, three little pets couldn't find what they want to buy. The teacher will read out the names of the things. Please complete the *pinyin* in the picture while listening to the teacher, and then help the little animals find what they want to buy according to the initial letters in their hands. After finding them, please raises your hand, and tell the teacher what these three animals want to buy.

___únzi ___īdàn ___ié ___úzi ___īguā ___iāngjiāo

7.3 Make fruit head decorations 制作水果头饰

Make a beautiful head decoration after the illustration. Keep it for use in singing for the next class.

8.1 Paint, write and speak 涂一涂，写一写，说一说

Two students are in a group. First paint the colors on their favorite fruits and drinks, and then write down the names in either *pinyin* or the Chinese characters. After that, write down your names, and then compare to see the similarities and the differences between their favorite fruits and drinks. Use “I eat/drink…” to make a dialogue.

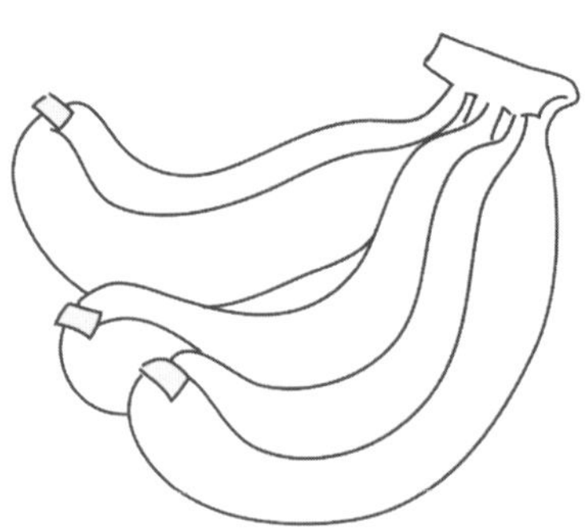

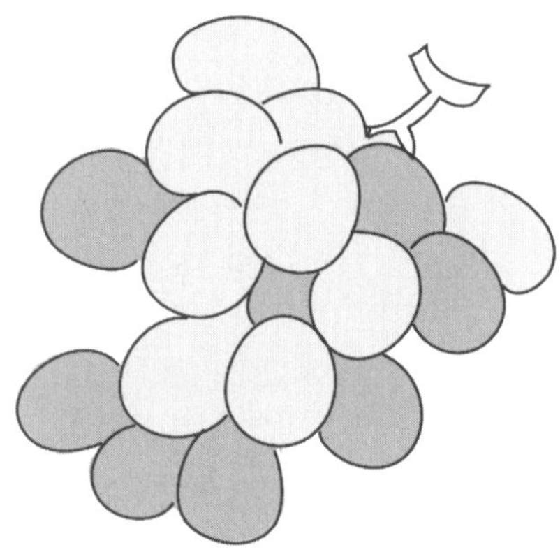

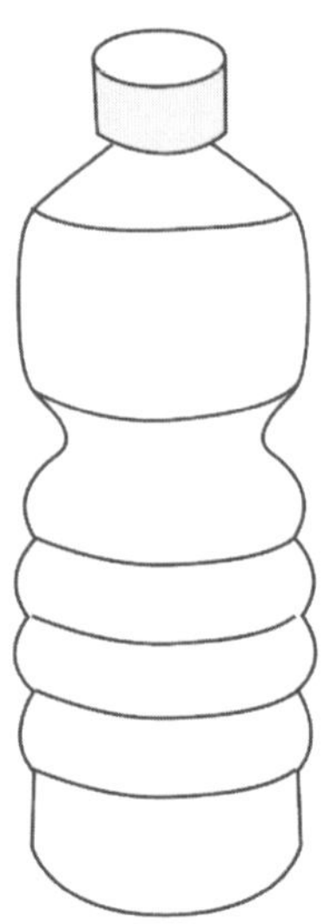

8.2 The fruit basket for the teacher 送给老师的水果篮

Please cut out the colored fruits from the Attachment 8.1 , and then paste them onto the fruit basket on the page and write your names in the fruit basket. After that, cut out the fruit basket and send it to your teacher. Please tell your teacher what fruits there are in the basket.

8.3 Ask and look for 问一问，找一找

Two students are in a group. One holds Picture A and one holds Picture B. You can't look at other's picture. There is only one person (or an animal) who likes the same fruits (or drinks) in the two pictures. All the others like different things. Please find the people (or animal) who like the same fruit (or drink) through the dialogue.

对话示例：A：杰克喜欢菠萝。
　　　　　B：杰克喜欢苹果。

9.1 Look and read 找一找，读一读

Find how many z, c, and s in the following children song in the shortest time possible. Write down these numbers in the blank circles under the children song. After done, raise your hand for your teacher's attention, and then read the song to the teacher.

一个字，两个字， yí gè zì liǎng gè zì	One word, two words,
三个字，四个字， sān gè zì sì gè zì	Three words, four words,
娃娃写了四个字。 wá wa xiě le sì gè zì	The little kid wrote four words.
擦呀擦，擦呀擦， cā ya cā cā ya cā	Erase, and erase,
娃娃擦掉两个字。 wá wa cā diào liǎng gè zì	The little kid erased two words.
剩下两个什么字？ shèng xià liǎng gè shén me zì	What are the two words left?
一个十，一个四。 yí gè shí yí gè sì	One is ten, and the other is four.

z ◯ c ◯ s ◯

9.2 Grab the cards 抢卡片

Listen to the teacher and grab the card with the word quickly and raise it up. If you take the right cards, you can keep them and continue the game. If you take the wrong cards, you have to exit from the game. In the end, who grabs the most cards wins.

在	卫生间
花园	客厅
书房	饭厅
厨房	卧室

9.3a Stick and paint 贴一贴，涂一涂

Cut out the pictures of the objects from the page, and then stick them in the different rooms according to your own ideas. Finally, paint them with beautiful colors. After that, introduce your works to your class.

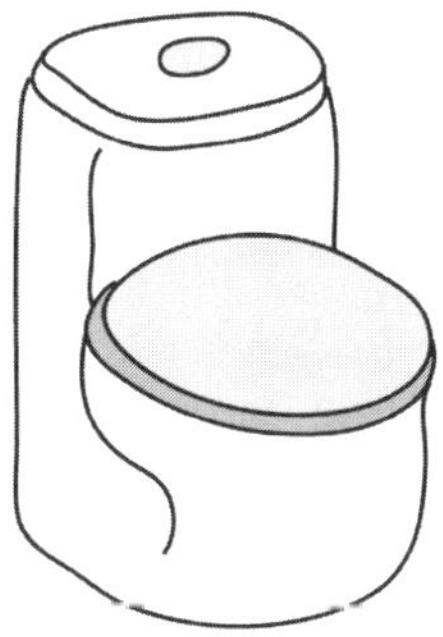

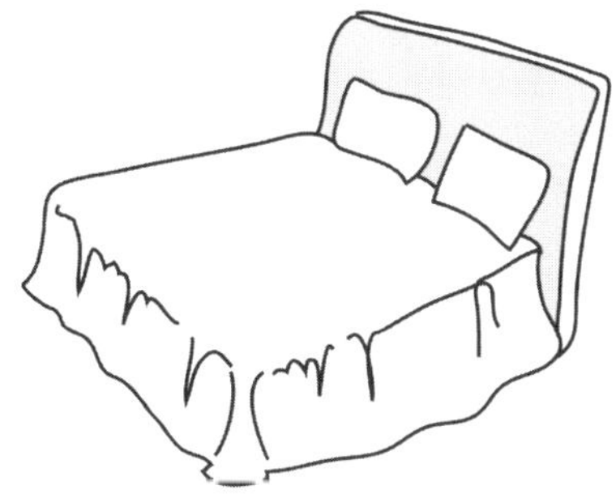

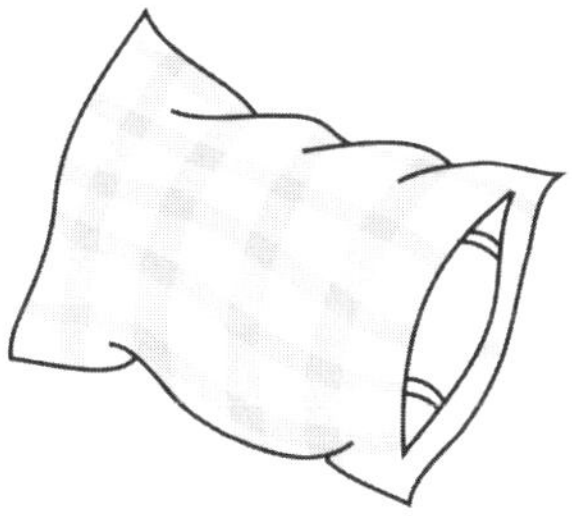
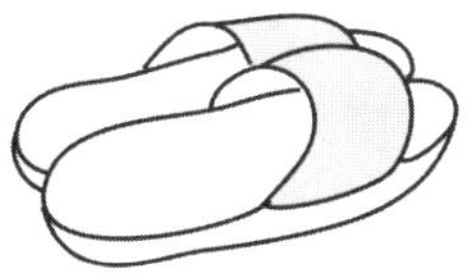
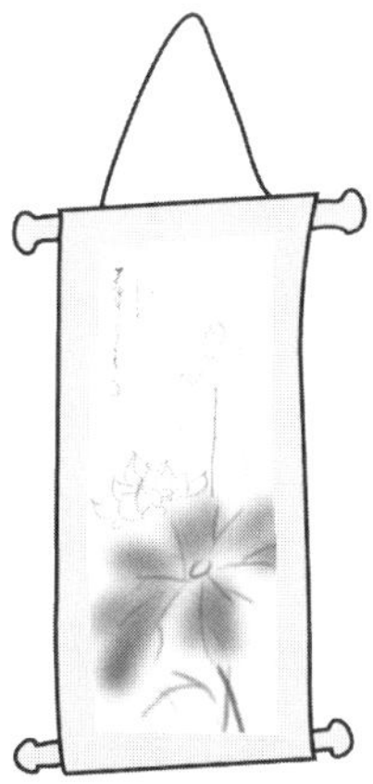
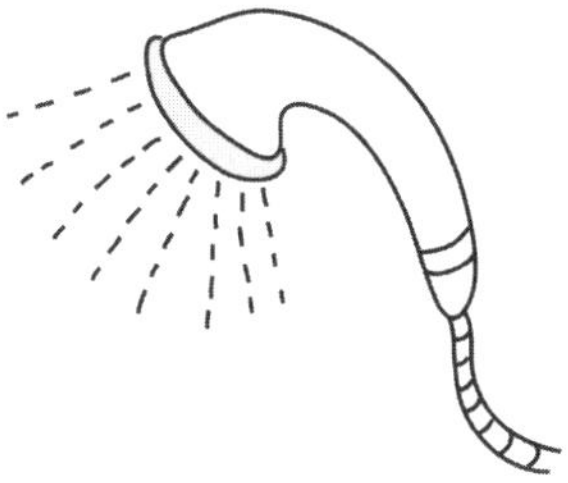

9.3b Stick and paint 贴一贴，涂一涂

卧室 wòshì	厨房 chúfáng
卫生间 wèishēngjiān	客厅 kètīng

10.2 Look for the same picture 找相同

Two students are in a group. One holds Picture A and the other holds Picture B. You can't look at each other's picture. There is only one drawing in each picture that is identical, and the rest of the drawings all have different places. Please find the identical drawings from the two pictures.

对话示例：A：美美在花园。
B：美美在客厅。

10.3 Quick memory 快速记忆

Several students are in a group. Try to memorize the contents of the nine small pictures in 30 seconds. Then give the Activity Pages back to the teacher. The teacher raises the cards and reads out their names in Chinese. Each group competes to answer where these people or animals are by their memory. The right answer gets one point; the wrong one gets no point. At the end of the game, the group with the most points wins.

11.2 Connect the words into lines 连词成线

Listen to the teacher and mark the serial numbers on the words heard. At the same time, make a tick at the same time. If you make the five words into a linear line or a slant one, please raises your hand to draw attention from the teacher. The student who connects the most linear lines or the slant lines wins in the end.

听音乐	唱歌	玩游戏	踢球	读书
跳舞	看电视	读书	听音乐	唱歌
玩游戏	踢球	听音乐	跳舞	看电视
读书	唱歌	看电视	玩游戏	跳舞
踢球	听音乐	读书	唱歌	玩游戏

11.3 Who has the birthday on the same day as someone else? 谁和谁的生日是同一天？

Two students are in a group. One student holds Picture A and the other holds Picture B. You can't see the other's picture. One student tells the other the birthday date on Picture A; the other then looks at Picture B to see if it has the same date on it. If it has, then use the color pen to paint the person's name on it. After checking everyone's birthday each group makes a calculation on how many people have birthdays on the same day on both Picture A and Picture B. Compete to see which group can finish the task fast and well.

句型示例：XX的生日是X月X号。

A

Ben 9月22号

Clare 1月30号

Tom 10月10号

John 7月15号

Chris 5月26号

Susan 11月4号

Alan 3月16号

Sharon 2月1号

B

Paul 7月15号

Adam 11月8号

Kate 3月16号

Jane 10月10号

Mary 2月1号

Mark 9月23号

Tony 5月26号

Peter 1月10号

12.1 Card game 卡片游戏

Several students are in one group and play a game with cards together. Each student can only turn over one card each time. If you can speak the names of the actions on the card, you can keep the card. Otherwise, you will have to put back the card on the desktop. After the game, the group that gets the most cards wins in the end.

12.2 Similar hobbies 相同的爱好

Two students are in a group. One holds Picture A and the other holds Picture B. You can't see the other's picture. One tells the other someone's hobby in his/her picture. The other looks for the person's name on his picture, who shares the similar hobbies. Then use the color pens to paint it over. Compete to see which group can finish the task fast and best.

参考句型：XX喜欢……

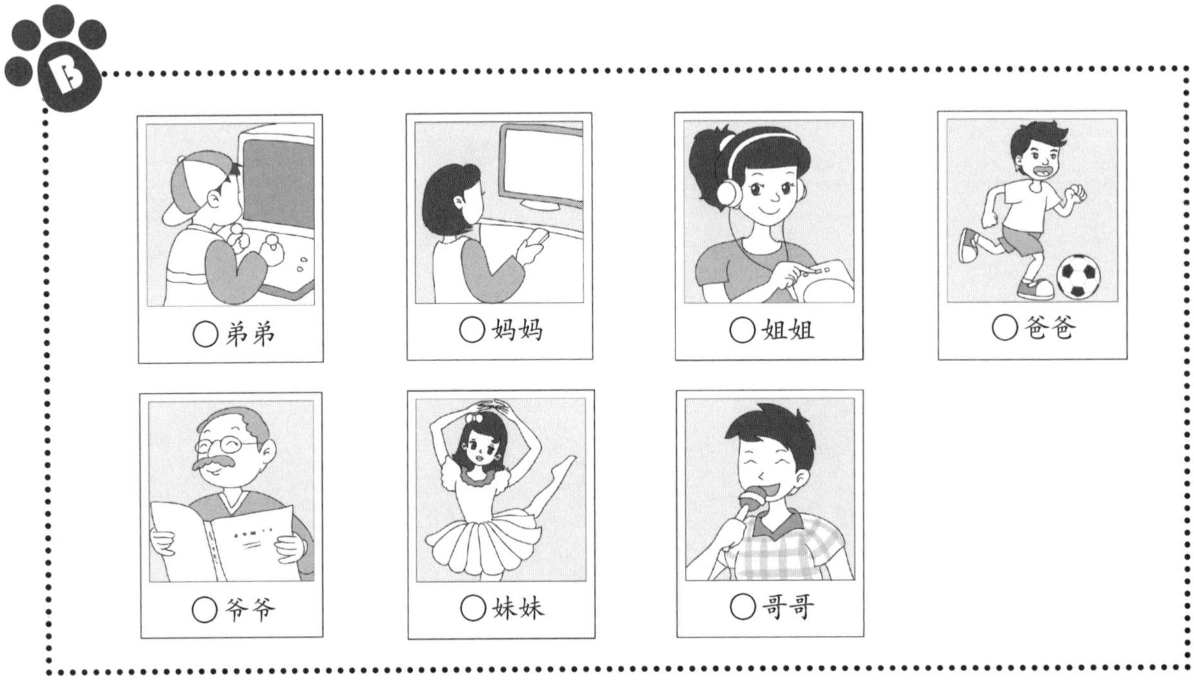

12.3 Connect the words into sentences 连词成句

Cut out the following words, and then write down your family members' or your close friends' names in the blank grids. Then arrange these words into five sentences. Compete to see who can finish the task fast and best.

听音乐	唱歌	玩游戏	读书
看电视	喜欢	喜欢	喜欢
喜欢	喜欢		

13.1 Look and read 找一找，读一读

Find how many y and w in the following children song in the shortest time. Write down these numbers in the blank circles under the children song. After done, raise your hand for your teacher's attention, and then read the song to the teacher.

一朵乌云飘过来， yì duǒ wū yún piāo guò lái	One piece of dark cloud floats over,
两朵乌云飘过来， liǎng duǒ wū yún piāo guò lái	Two pieces of dark cloud float over,
三朵乌云飘过来， sān duǒ wū yún piāo guò lái	Three pieces of dark cloud float over,
四朵乌云飘过来， sì duǒ wū yún piāo guò lái	Four pieces of dark cloud float over,
五朵乌云飘过来， wǔ duǒ wū yún piāo guò lái	Five pieces of dark cloud float over,
六朵乌云飘过来， liù duǒ wū yún piāo guò lái	Six pieces of dark cloud float over,
太阳被云遮住了， tài yáng bèi yún zhē zhù le	The Sun is covered by the dark clouds,
天上开始下雨了。 tiān shàng kāi shǐ xià yǔ le	It begins to rain.

y ○　　　w ○

13.3 Look for objects 找物品

First cut out the objects from the picture, and then stick them in the right circles. Compete to see who can finish the task fast and well.

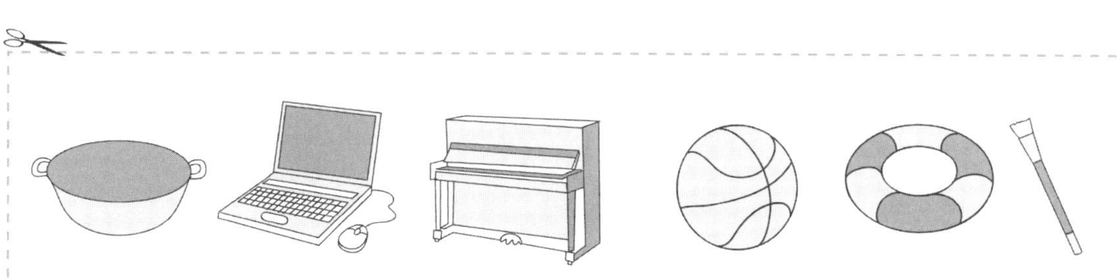

14.1 Make small paper box 制作小纸盒

First cut out the pictures along the dotted line with scissors, then fold the pictures along the dotted line, finally, stick the edges together to make a small paper box. After that, two persons are in a group. One throws a paper box, and then uses the color pencils to make a mark on the up-facing side, and then makes up a sentence based on the picture on this side: "他/她会……" Each paper box has six sides. Each person has ten chances to throw the paper box. The person with the most number of the same sides with ten throws wins in the end.

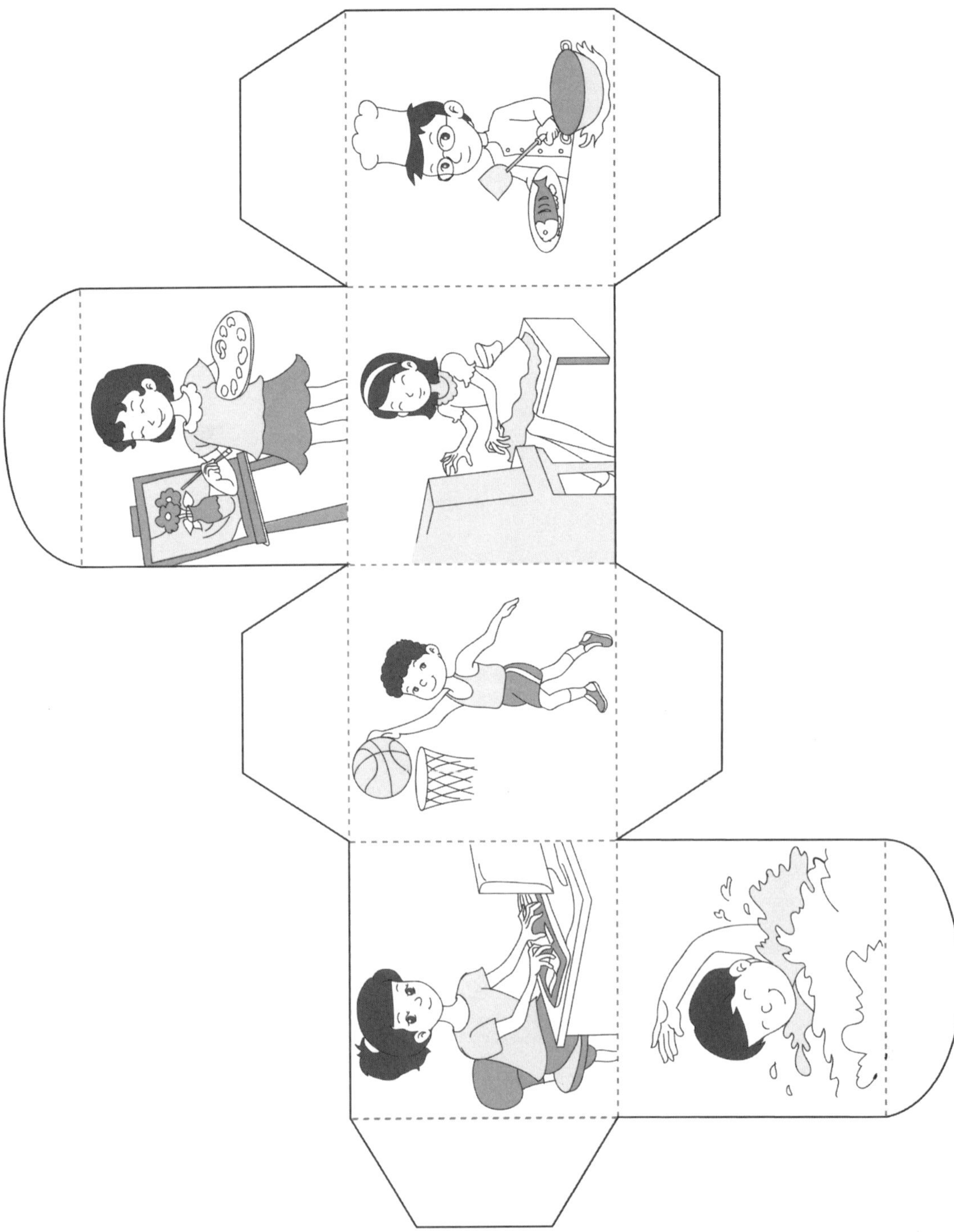

14.2 卡片游戏

Several persons are in a group. Each group elects a group leader who gets two sets of the cards. The group leader puts the cards face down on their desktop. Members in each group say one thing they can do in turn, for example, "我会游泳". After that you turns over one card. If the card has the same words as you has said, you can keep the card; if not, you have to put back the card on the desktop. Then the group leader reshuffles the cards. The next member starts to say the sentences. Each member has five chances to speak and turn over the cards. At the end of the game, the member with the most cards wins.

15.1 Listen to the teacher and fill in the chart 听音填表

Listen to the teacher and find the corresponding positions for the syllables according to the teacher's reading of the initial and final sounds. After that, they can write out the syllables at the location, or write out the tonal marks. Compete to see who can finish the task fast and well.

	a	o	e	i	u	ü	an	ao	ang	en	eng	ie	ei	ou	uo	in	ing	iang
b																		
p																		
d																		
t																		
g																		
k																		
h																		
m																		
n																		
l																		
j																		
q																		
x																		
f																		
z																		
c																		
s																		
ch																		
zh																		
sh																		
r																		
y																		
w																		

15.2 Word matching game 组词游戏

Cut out the following characters, and then put the characters into the correct city names, and finally, stick them to the corresponding pictures of the cities. After done, they raise your hands to get teacher's attention. Read the names of the cities to your teacher.

上	昆	北	明	港	海	香	京

16.1 Great Wall puzzle 长城拼图

Paint the big picture with beautiful colors, and then cut it up into small pieces along the dotted line. Reference the miniature picture of the Great Wall on the Activity Page; piece together the small puzzles into a complete picture of the Great Wall. Compete to see who can finish the task fast and best.

16.2 Throw dice 掷色子

Several persons are in a group. Throw dice in turn, and then move your chess pieces according to the number on the dice. The person who reaches the destination first wins in the end.

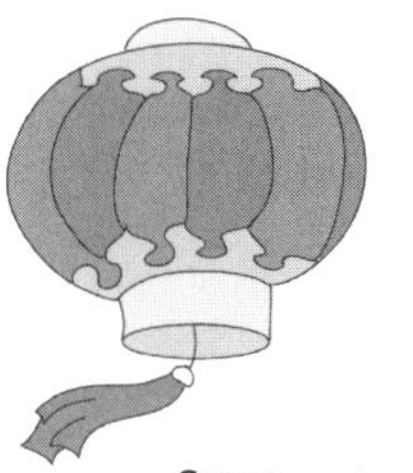 Start →	1 Read the number	2 Read the number	 What's this?	4 Read the number
9 Read the number	中国 Read the word	7 Read the number		5 Read the number
10 Read the number	11 Read the number		13 Read the number	北京 Read the word
19 Read the number	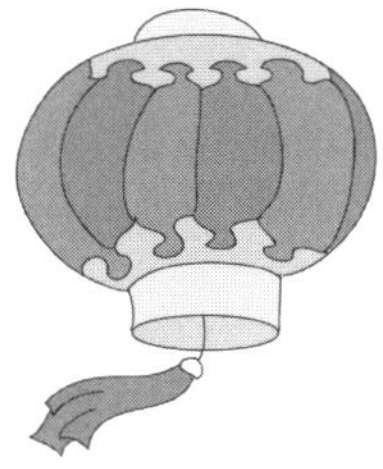	17 Read the number		15 Read the number
	21 Read the number		23 Read the number	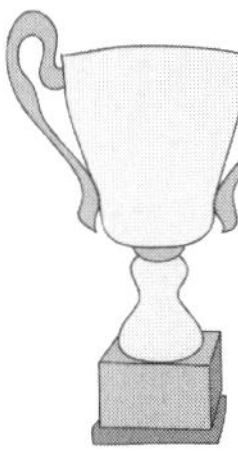 End

汉语拼音方案

一、字母表

字母	名称	字母	名称	字母	名称
Aa	ㄚ	Jj	ㄐㄧㄝ	Ss	ㄝㄙ
Bb	ㄅㄝ	Kk	ㄎㄝ	Tt	ㄊㄝ
Cc	ㄘㄝ	Ll	ㄝㄌ	Uu	ㄨ
Dd	ㄉㄝ	Mm	ㄝㄇ	Vv	□ㄝ
Ee	ㄜ	Nn	ㄋㄝ	Ww	ㄨㄚ
Ff	ㄝㄈ	Oo	ㄛ	Xx	ㄒㄧ
Gg	ㄍㄝ	Pp	ㄆㄝ	Yy	ㄧㄚ
Hh	ㄏㄚ	Qq	ㄑㄧㄡ	Zz	ㄗㄝ
Ii	ㄧ	Rr	ㄚㄦ		

v只用来拼写外来语、少数民族语言和方言。

字母的手写体依照拉丁字母的一般书写习惯。

二、声母表

b	p	m	f	d	t	n	l
ㄅ玻	ㄆ坡	ㄇ摸	ㄈ佛	ㄉ得	ㄊ特	ㄋ讷	ㄌ勒

g	k	h	j	q	x
ㄍ哥	ㄎ科	ㄏ喝	ㄐ基	ㄑ欺	ㄒ希

zh	ch	sh	r	z	c	s
ㄓ知	ㄔ蚩	ㄕ诗	ㄖ日	ㄗ资	ㄘ雌	ㄙ思

在给汉字注音的时候，为了使拼式简短，zh ch sh 可以省作 ẑ ĉ ŝ。

三、韵母表

	i 丨 衣	u ㄨ 乌	ü ㄩ 迂
a ㄚ 啊	ia 丨ㄚ 呀	ua ㄨㄚ 蛙	
o ㄛ 喔		uo ㄨㄛ 窝	
e ㄜ 鹅	ie 丨ㄝ 耶		üe ㄩㄝ 约
ai ㄞ 哀		uai ㄨㄞ 歪	
ei ㄟ 诶		uei ㄨㄟ 威	
ao ㄠ 熬	iao 丨ㄠ 腰		
ou ㄡ 欧	iou 丨ㄡ 忧		
an ㄢ 安	ian 丨ㄢ 烟	uan ㄨㄢ 弯	üan ㄩㄢ 冤
en ㄣ 恩	in 丨ㄣ 因	uen ㄨㄣ 温	ün ㄩㄣ 晕
ang ㄤ 昂	iang 丨ㄤ 央	uang ㄨㄤ 汪	
eng ㄥ 亨的韵母	ing 丨ㄥ 英	ueng ㄨㄥ 翁	
ong ㄨㄥ轰的韵母	iong ㄩㄥ 雍		

（1）“知、蚩、诗、日、资、雌、思”等七个音节的韵母用i，即：知、蚩、诗、日、资、雌、思等字拼作zhi，chi，shi，ri，zi，ci，si。

（2）韵母儿写成er，用做韵尾的时候写成r。例如：“儿童”拼作ertong，“花儿”拼作huār。

（3）韵母ㄝ单用的时候写成ê。

（4）i行的韵母，前面没有声母的时候，写成：yi（衣），ya（呀），ye（耶），yao（腰），you（忧），yan（烟），yin（因），yang（央），ying（英），yong（雍）。

u行的韵母，前面没有声母的时候，写成wu（乌），wa（蛙），wo（窝），wai（歪），wei（威），wan（弯），wen（温），wang（汪），weng（翁）。

ü行的韵母，前面没有声母的时候，写成yu（迂），yue（约），yuan（冤），yun（晕）；ü上两点省略。

ü行的韵母跟声母j，q，x拼的时候，写成ju（居），qu（区），xu（虚），ü上两点也省略；但是跟声母l，n拼的时候，仍然写成lü（吕），nü（女）。

（5）iou，uei，uen前面加声母的时候，写成：iu，ui，un。例如niu（牛），gui（归），lun（论）。

（6）在给汉字注音的时候，为了使拼式简短，ng可以省作ŋ。

四、声调符号

阴平	阳平	上声	去声
ˉ	ˊ	ˇ	ˋ

声调符号标在音节的主要母音上。轻声不标。例如：

妈 mā	麻 má	马 mǎ	骂 mà	吗 ma
阴平	阳平	上声	去声	轻声

五、隔音符号

a，o，e开头的音节连接在其他音节后面的时候，如果音节的界限发生混淆，用隔音符号（’）隔开，例如pi’ao（皮袄）。

汉字笔画名称表

类别	序号	笔形	名称	例字
基本笔形	1	㇐	横	十
	2	㇑	竖	中
	3	㇒	撇	八
	4	㇔	点	主
	5	㇏	捺	人
	6	㇀	提	地
派生笔形	7	㇕	横折	口
	8	㇇	横撇	又
	9	㇖	横钩	写
	10	㇆	横折钩	月
	11	㇊	横折提	记
	12	㇍	横折弯	朵
	13	㇅	横折折	凹
	14	㇠	横折斜钩	飞
	15	㇈	横折弯钩	九
	16	㇌	横撇弯钩	队
	17	㇋	横折折撇	及
	18	㇡	横折折折钩	乃
	19	㇎	横折折折	凸
	20	㇙	竖提	民
	21	㇗	竖折	山
	22	㇚	竖钩	小
	23	㇄	竖弯	四
	24	㇟	竖弯钩	儿
	25	ㄣ	竖折撇	专
	26	㇞	竖折折	鼎
	27	㇉	竖折折钩	马
	28	㇛	撇点	女
	29	㇜	撇折	么
	30	㇂	斜钩	我
	31	㇁	弯钩	家

汉字常用偏旁名称表

部首	偏旁	例字	部首	偏旁	例字
刂	立刀旁	刮、划、刺、刷	王	王字旁	球、班、现、玩
亻	单立人旁	做、他、们、什	木	木字旁	板、机、林、杯
冫	两点水	冷、净、冰、决	日	日字旁	明、昨、晴、晚
讠	言字旁	认、语、识、读	贝	贝字旁	员、财、贴、败
阝	右耳刀旁	郑、郎、都、邓	攵	反文旁	故、放、数、敌
土	提土旁	地、场、塔、坏	火	火字旁	炒、烤、灯、灿
扌	提手旁	打、拖、报、排	灬	四点底	点、照、熊、然
口	口字旁	叫、吃、吗、呢	礻	示补旁	礼、视、祝、神
囗	口字框	国、园、图、困	石	石字旁	碗、砍、砖、研
犭	反犬旁	狗、猫、狮、猴	目	目字旁	眼、睛、睡、盼
夕	夕字旁	名、多、岁、梦	钅	金字旁	银、针、锅、铁
饣	食字旁	饭、饺、饿、饮	禾	禾字旁	租、和、秋、种
广	广字旁	应、店、座、床	疒	病字旁	疼、疾、病、疗
氵	三点水旁	汁、漂、游、泳	穴	穴宝盖	穿、穷、突、窗
忄	竖心旁	快、忆、忙、怀	页	页字旁	颐、预、顿、顶
宀	宝盖头	它、家、客、宝	竹	竹字头	笔、篮、筷、筒
辶	走之旁	边、过、遍、进	走	走字旁	起、超、赵、赶
女	女字旁	妈、妹、姐、好	𧾷	足字旁	跳、跟、跨、趴
马	马字旁	驯、骑、驰、驶	雨	雨字头	雪、雷、需、雾
纟	绞丝旁	红、绿、绘、结			

汉字笔顺规则表

类别	序号	规　　则	例　　字
基本规则	1	先横反竖	十十
	2	先撇后捺	人人
	3	从上到下	三三三
	4	从左到右	仁仁仁仁
	5	先外后里	问问问问问问
	6	先外后里再封口	国国国国国国国国
	7	先中间后两边	小小小
补充规则	1	点在上部或左上，先写	衣衣衣衣衣衣/为为为为
	2	点在右上或字里，后写	发发发发发/瓦瓦瓦瓦
	3	上右和上左包围结构，先外后里	司司司司司/斤斤斤斤
	4	左下包围结构，先里后外	远远远远远远远
	5	左下右包围结构，先里后外	凶凶凶凶
	6	左上右包围结构，先外后里	同同同同同同
	7	上左下包围结构，先上后里再左下	区区区区

汉字形体结构类型表

现代汉字的间架结构，可以分为五大类型、十三种。五大类型是：独体、左右、上下、包围和对称。十三种结构形式是：独体、左右、左中右、上下、上中下、上左包围、上右包围、左下包围、左上右包围、上左下包围、左下右包围、全包围、对称。现略加归并，图示如下：

1. 独体字结构

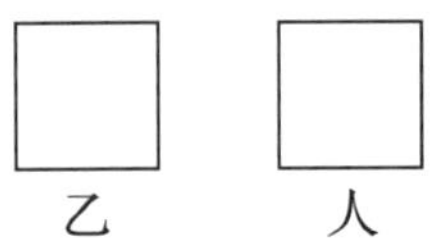

2. 左右结构（含左中右结构）

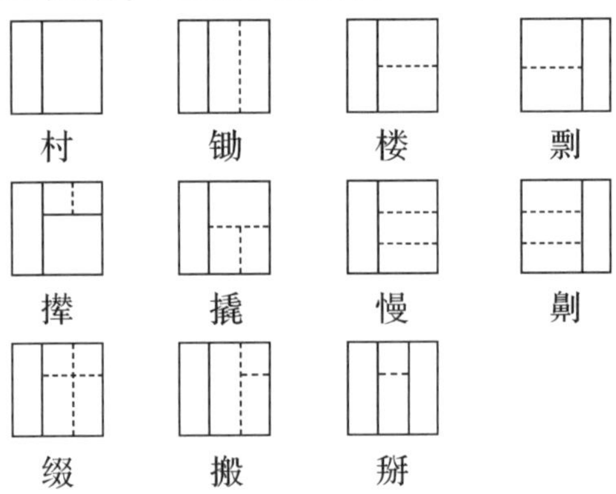

3. 上下结构（含上中下结构）

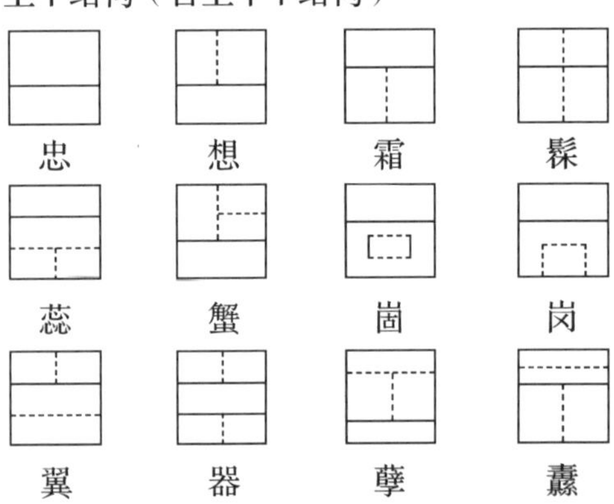

4. 上左包围结构

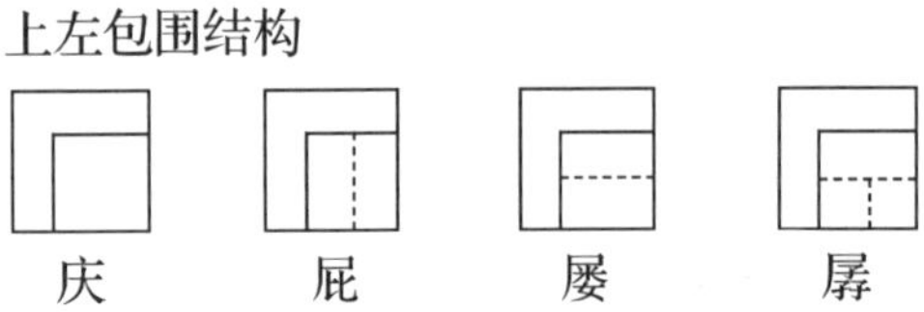

5. 上右包围结构

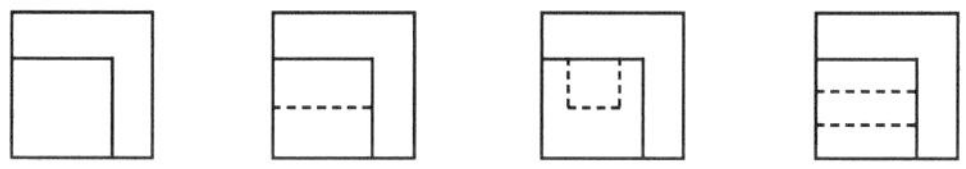

句　虱　匈　匐

6. 左下包围结构

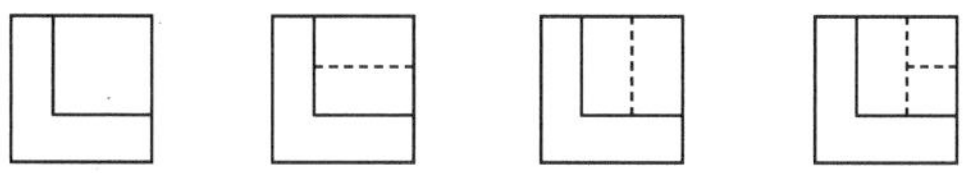

延　毯　迦　邂

7. 左上右包围结构

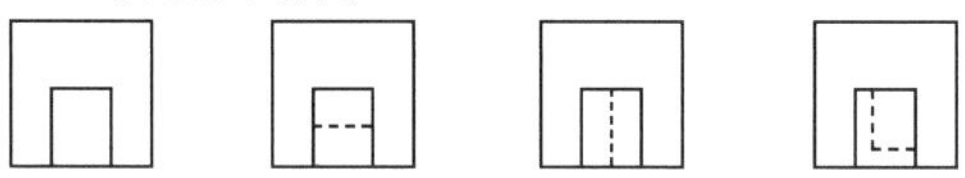

风　周　网　闳

8. 上左下包围结构

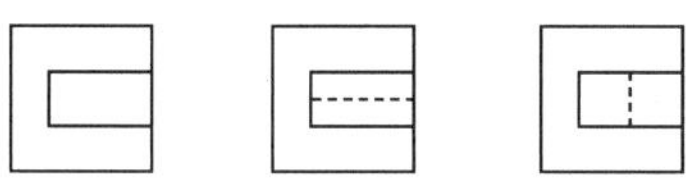

区　匿　瓯

9. 左下右包围结构

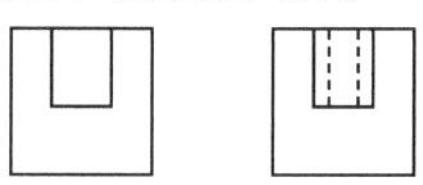

凶　函

10. 全包围结构

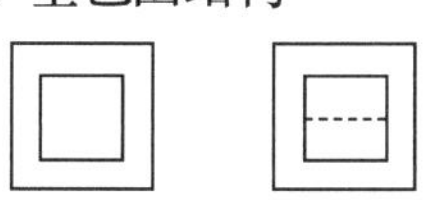

国　圆

11. 对称结构

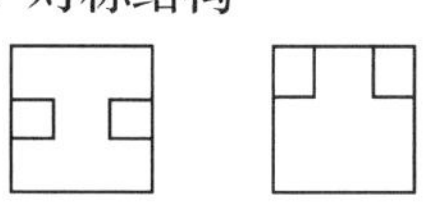

乘　坐

	a	o	e	er	ai	ei	un	uang	ueng	ü	üe	üan	ün
	a	o	e	er	ai	ei							
b	ba	bo			bai	be							
p	pa	po			pai	pe							
m	ma	mo	me		mai	m							
f	fa	fo				fe							
d	da		de		dai	de	dun						
t	ta		te		tai		tun						
n	na		ne		nai	ne				nü	nüe		
l	la		le		lai	lei	lun			lü	lüe		
z	za		ze		zai	ze	zun						
c	ca		ce		cai		cun						
s	sa		se		sai		sun						
zh	zha		zhe		zhai	zh	zhun	zhuang					
ch	cha		che		chai	ch	chun	chuang					
sh	sha		she		shai	sh	shun	shuang					
r			re				run						
j										ju	jue	juan	jun
q										qu	que	quan	qun
x										xu	xue	xuan	xun
g	ga		ge		gai	g	gun	guang					
k	ka		ke		kai	ke	kun	kuang					
h	ha		he		hai	he	hun	huang					
y										yu	yue	yuan	yun
w							wen	wang	weng				

郑重声明

高等教育出版社依法对本书享有专有出版权。任何未经许可的复制、销售行为均违反《中华人民共和国著作权法》，其行为人将承担相应的民事责任和行政责任，构成犯罪的，将被依法追究刑事责任。为了维护市场秩序，保护读者的合法权益，避免读者误用盗版书造成不良后果，我社将配合行政执法部门和司法机关对违法犯罪的单位和个人给予严厉打击。社会各界人士如发现上述侵权行为，希望及时举报，本社将奖励举报有功人员。

反盗版举报电话： (010) 58581897/58581896/58581879

反盗版举报传真： (010) 82086060

E - mail： dd@hep.com.cn

通信地址： 北京市西城区德外大街4号
高等教育出版社打击盗版办公室

邮　　编： 100120

购书请拨打电话： (010)58581118